Forgotten Neighborhood Games

Get Kids Back Outside and Loving It!

By

Scott Strother

© 2004 by Scott Strother. All rights reserved.

No part of this book may be reproduced, stored in a retrieval system, or transmitted by any means, electronic, mechanical, photocopying, recording, or otherwise, without written permission from the author.

First published by AuthorHouse 04/08/04

ISBN: 1-4140-6205-2 (e-book)
ISBN: 1-4184-2226-6 (Paperback)

This book is printed on acid free paper.

Table of Contents

Preface ix

Introduction xi

Picking the "It" xiii

Activity Level V 1
    Ball Tag 2
    Balloon Volley 3
    Keep-Away Volleyball 3
    Bombardment 4
    Broom Chaser 5
    Capture the Colors 6
    Capture the Flag 7
    Jailbreak 8
    Prisoner's Base 8
    Chain Tag 9
    Change Dodgeball 10
    Chinese Tag 11
    Circle Pass 12
    Circle Survivor 13
    Basketball Circle Survivor 13
    Combination/Creative Tag 14
    Crack the Whip 15
    Dodgeball 16
    Doctor Dodgeball 16
    Free For All Dodgeball 17
    Alley Dodgeball 17
    Square Dodgeball 17
    Flashlight Tag 18
    Frisbee$_{TM}$ War 19
    Interference Tag 20
    Jack, Jack, Show Your Light 21
    Jump Rope 22

Keep Away Chase 23
King (or Queen) of the Hill 24
Kings and Queens 25
Mini-Tennis 26
Mulberry Bush 27
Nutmeg 28
Obstacle Course 29
Races 30
Reverse Tag 31
Scorpion Tag 32
Skrag 33
Small Hockey 34
Roller Hockey 35
Broom Hockey 35
Small Soccer 36
Tail-Grabbers 37
Thirty-Two Tips 38
Three Court Soccer 39
Touch Football 40
One Chance Football 40
Ultimate Frisbee$_{TM}$ 41
Boundary Ball 41
Water Fights 42
You're Under Arrest! 43

Activity Level IV 45

Base Rush 46
British Bulldog 47
Category Tag 48
Sit-down Tag 48
Cats in the Corner 49
Chicago 50
Club Ball 51
Dare Goal 52
Follow the Leader 53
Four Corners 54
Army-Navy 54
Scramble 54

Fox and Geese 55
Freeze Tag 56
Tunnel Tag 56
Hit or Run 57
Hot Box 58
Infiltration 59
Last Man Tag 61
Link Tag 62
No Touch Ground 63
Red Light, Green Light 64
Relays 65
Rim Game 66
Roof Game 68
Spinning Rope 69
Sprite Ball 70
Statues 71
Red Light, Green Light Statues 71
Steal the Bacon 72
Stride Club Bowl 73
Standing Nutmeg 74
Brooklyn Bridge 74
Tiger and Leopard 75
Two-Man Basketball 76
Wall Ball 77

Activity Level III 79

1, 2, 3…I spy 80
Army 82
Ball Punch 83
Break and Run 84
Keeper and Bull 84
Circle Chase 85
Cowboys and Indians 86
Ghost in the Graveyard 87
Kick the Can 88
Manhunt 89
Ringalevio 90
Maypole 91

One Man Toss Up	92
Pass and Overtake	93
Peg	94
Red Devil	96
Sardines	97
Slap the Nose	98
Spud	99
Buddy Spud	100
Call Ball	100
Stoop Ball	101
Swat Tag	103
Ten Ball	104
What's the Time Mr. Wolf?	105

Activity Level II 107

500	108
Attack	109
Buck, Buck	110
Crossing the Brook	111
Exchange	112
Four Square	113
Paddle Four Square	114
Two Square	114
Garage Ball Tag	115
Hand Slap	116
Hide and Seek	117
Hopscotch	118
Indian Wrestling	119
Log Roll	120
Monkey in the Middle	121
Keep Away	121
Palm Boxing	122
Poison Circle	123
Prisoner's Attack	124
Red Rover	125
Treasure Hunt	126
Tug of War	127

Activity Level I 129

- Around the World 130
- Bean Bag Toss 131
- Bocce 132
- Building 133
- Circle Target Bowl 134
- Multiple Target Throw 134
- Cornhole 135
- Deadbox 136
- Down Down Down 137
- Frisbee$_{TM}$ Golf 138
- Soccer Golf 138
- Homerun Derby 139
- Horse 140
- Jacks 141
- Lawn Darts 142
- Lawn Golf 143
- Line Club Bowl 144
- Stake Target Bowl 144
- Long Ball 145
- Marbles 146
- Mother May I 147
- Paper Plane Contest 148
- Pottsie 149
- Rears Up 150
- Soccer Croquet 151
- Throw for Distance 152
- Untangle 153
- Water Balloon Toss 154

References 155

Preface

Two powerful motives inspired me to create this book. These are two issues that people seem to realize, but never really stop to ponder. The first inspiration came over the last few summers that I worked as a tennis coach and instructor. I taught kids ages six to sixteen (the children that will get the most use from this book). The children and I would have fun together, especially when I taught them creative tennis games. One day, I began talking to a few of my students about other fun games I use to play around my neighborhood. You would not believe the blank stares of bewilderment that lay upon me as I mentioned 'Ghost in the Graveyard' and even 'Kick the Can'. This was too much for me to handle. Why? I will come to that shortly.

The second inspiration came while writing a paper on childhood obesity. In the back of my mind, I had always noticed what seemed to be an increase in this problem, but never paid too much attention to it. As I researched this topic, I was amazed on how bad the problem really has become. I will not bore you with the lengthy facts and details, but childhood obesity is reaching epidemic proportions. This is partially due to the increase in fast food and video games that cause a lack of exercise, poor food choices, and overall decreased health. The adverse effects of childhood obesity are too strong to be ignored.

The combination of this dilemma and children's unawareness of these outdoor games felt like a smack in the face. The games in this book are simply too much fun and offer too many positive rewards to be set aside for video games. It bothers me to think that kids are not outside enjoying them.

Let me briefly describe my childhood and it might help to explain my enthusiasm for the games included in this book. I grew up in a neighborhood which I loved tremendously. This is mostly due to the activities in which I found myself involved. Every night after dinner, and often during the day, kids from all over the neighborhood would come out and gather near my house. If people did not meet, we would go out and find anyone and everyone. Each time, we would all organize a large game for everyone to play. I will not discuss which games (because they are all described in this book!), but I loved them all. It was not just the games, but getting together with friends, making new friends, exercising, being outside, *and* doing a fun activity that made the process so enjoyable. Other kids felt the exact same way. This is why no one could stay away.

The more I thought about how much fun I used to have, the more amazed I was that many kids are not enjoying these activities. When I look back upon growing up, these games are a large part of my memories. Once children get into a routine of playing the games in this book, it should elate them as it did me. Even if children already know some games, this book offers an enormous variety of new, exciting games that children can learn and play.

I want all children to share in the positive memories that I had. Learning and playing these games will be great for kids in more ways than you can imagine. It might take a little effort at first, learning the games and getting other children to play, but once kids start learning these exciting games, they will not want to stop. Do not be afraid to go find kids and coerce them outside for some fun. More and more children from the neighborhood will start to get involved. Everyone will begin looking forward to playing and will meet more often. Instead of sitting around inside, kids can meet each other, make friends, get exercise, and have a ton of fun! This is what childhood is all about. Kids need to get back outside, exercise, and love it…and this book is the guide!

Introduction

This book is divided into five Activity Levels. This organization is to help children easily select a game depending on their mood and how much exercise they desire. The amount of exercise that can be expected from each game is defined below.

Activity Level V: This level includes games that require the most exercise. These games mainly entail constant running or movement and are highly active.

Activity Level IV: This level includes games that are also highly active. These games are more likely to include short breaks in the action, but mostly constant movement or running will be involved.

Activity Level III: This level includes games where running is involved, but it is definitely not constant. There will be slows points in the game where players can rest, but everyone will still get good exercise.

Activity Level II: This level includes games where little running is required. Games may include briefs periods of running with mostly stationary activity or may require less demanding physical activity.

Activity Level I: This level includes games where mostly walking or limited physical exercise is required. These games are still active and outside, but are not as physically demanding as the others.

I highly suggest searching all the Activity Levels for every child. Even children who only wish to run constantly or children who hate to run will find enjoyable games within each Activity Level. There are fantastic games to explore throughout this book, so use it to the fullest and try them all!

One word of caution must also be said before children begin to play these games. Some of the games involve physical contact and almost all require physical activity. There is some risk of getting injured, especially if the rules are not followed and standard safety cautions are ignored. Please be sure to follow the rules as they are stated and do not add extra physical contact. Also, where safety equipment could be utilized, be encouraged to use it. Guidance and supervision are wonderful tools that should be used, especially when children are learning a new game. Parents should help children fully understand the game and can watch to ensure no dangerous activities are occurring. These games are highly enjoyable, but will be even more fun if no one gets hurt!

One last item everyone needs to know before getting started is how to pick the "It". In numerous games below, one or more players will need to be chosen to play a certain role, often referred to as the "It". *Picking the "It"* describes commonly used methods in how to choose this player. This guide may be followed or players can create their own method.

Picking the "It"

This process will be useful for choosing the "It" in numerous games encountered in this book. Picking the "It" in these methods can be almost as entertaining as the game itself. It is important for players to mix up how "It" is chosen by trying out several of these methods.

For this process, everyone should always begin in a circle. One player will then choose the method of how the "It" will be picked. This player controls the action. Everyone in the circle holds out one or two hands. To choose the "It", the controlling player will go around the circle touching everyone's hands, one at a time, while saying a chant. Certain chants have traditionally been used and several of them are listed below. The controlling player begins by tapping the hand to his or her left and rotates clockwise around the circle. With each piece of the chant (one word or phrase), the controlling player taps the next player's hand and continues around the circle until the chant ends. The player in control must include his or her own hand in the tapping as well. When the chant ends, that last hand tapped is "landed on". If further rounds are played, the hand after the one "landed on" will be the first tapped in the next chant.

A single round can be performed where the person who is "landed on" becomes the "It".

The more common and exciting process is when the person "landed on" is safe and steps out of the circle. This continues until one person is left and becomes the "It".

A third way to perform this task is an elaborated version of the second method. Each person puts two hands in the circle. Each hand is counted and the hand that is "landed on" is taken out. When a player's hands are both out, that player can be deemed safe or "It" depending upon the rules decided.

I've even played a longer version where both fists are put in the middle. In this method, the first time a hand is "landed on", it turns into a flat hand, and the next time, it is eliminated. When a player's hands are both out, that player can be deemed safe or "It" depending upon the rules decided.

Here are some favorite chants we used to choose the "It", but players can feel free to make up their own as well.

One potato…:

One potato, two potato, three potato, four.
Five potato, six potato, seven potato, more.

The hand that is touched when "more" is said is "landed on".

Eeny Meeny:

Eeny, meeny, miny, moe.
Catch a tiger by the toe.
If he hollers let him go.
Eeny, meeny, miny, moe.

The hand that is touched when "moe" is said is "landed on".

Bubble Gum:

Bubble gum, bubble gum, in a dish.
How many pieces do you wish?

[The player landed on with "wish" says a number. That many hands are then tapped around the circle and the chant continues with one of the generic endings*. For example if the player said 4, this could be chanted]:

"1, 2, 3, 4, and you are out you dirty old dish rag turned inside out".

Only the hand that is touched when the last word of the generic ending is said is "landed on".

Engine Engine:

Engine, engine, number nine,
Going down Chicago line
If the train falls off the track
Do you want your money back?

[The person "landed on" with "back" picks "yes" or "no". Then the chant continues]:

Y, E, S, spells yes and you shall have your money back.
Or
N, O, spells no and you won't have your money back.

A hand is then officially "landed on" with the word "back".

My Mother and Your Mother:

My mother and your mother were at the store.
Your mother punched my mother in the nose.
What color was the blood?

[The player "landed on" names any color. This color is then spelled out and a generic ending* is added. For example, if "blue" is said]:

B, L, U, E, spells blue and my mother told me to pick the very best one and you are It.

Only the hand that is touched when the last word of the generic ending is said is "landed on".

Inca Binka:

Inka Binka bottle of inka,
The cork fell off and you stinka,
Not cause you're dirty,
Not 'cause you're clean,
Cause ya kissed a (boy or girl)
Behind a magazine
[add generic ending].

The hand that is touched when the last word of the generic ending is said is "landed on".

*Generic Endings:

And my mother told me to choose the very best one, and you are It.

And you are not It you dirty old dish rag turned in-side out.

And you are It.

Activity Level V

Ball Tag

Number of kids: 2 or more

Ages: any

Time allotted: 15 minutes or more

Space /Area: a grassy area or yard, preferably with some obstacles

Equipment: one soft ball, such as a playground or beach ball

Description:

Startup: Players should select a ball, define boundaries, and choose an "It".

Object: To avoid being It.

Play: Everyone spreads out in bounds. The It counts out loud to a certain number and the game begins. When the It has finished counting, play begins. The It then attempts to hit anyone with the ball. If the It is successful in hitting another player with the ball, that player becomes the It and play continues. Players may run and dodge the ball in any way they choose. They may also catch the ball to avoid becoming it. If the ball is caught, it is set on the ground and play resumes. The game continues until the players agree to quit.

Personal comments: A classic: simple and fun. Seems too simple and dull, but can be very intense. Once kids get into it, this game can provide quality entertainment for a good amount of time!

Balloon Volley[3]

Number of kids: 2 teams of 2 or more; or 1 on 1

Ages: any

Time allotted: 30 minutes or more

Space /Area: a large open field

Equipment: one or more balloons (depending on the number of players)

Description:

Startup: Players should define a playing field with goal lines on each end and choose teams.

Object: To score points by hitting the balloon(s) over the opponent's goal line.

Play: Each team scatters itself in the field as desired. The balloon or balloons are tossed into the air in the middle of the field and play begins. Players must never catch or hold the balloon, but may bat or kick it in any other way. A player or team scores one point for hitting a balloon over the opponent's goal line. No rough play or physical contact is allowed. Play continues until each balloon has been hit over a goal line. Then all balloons are brought back into the middle and a new round begins as before. The team who scores a given number of points first is the winner or the team with the most points after a certain number of rounds is the winner.

Personal Comments: Very simple, but very fun. Younger kids and some older kids will get a kick out of this. Fun to watch and play. Try it!

Variant: Keep-Away Volleyball[3]:
This is the same game except one volleyball is used instead of several balloons. Kicking is not allowed and a larger field should also be used. If the volleyball hits the ground, a toss up ensues and play continues. This takes a little more skill and teamwork than Balloon Volley, but is equally fun!

Bombardment (also called Pin Dodgeball)

Number of Kids: 2 teams of 3 or more

Ages: 7 and up

Time allotted: 40 minutes or more

Space /Area: a grass or black top area that can be split into two even sides

Equipment: playground balls (usually 2 or 3 depending upon the number of players), and however many "pins" are desired (usually 4-10 per team) (cones, tennis ball cans, etc. can be substituted for bowling pins)

Description:

Startup: Players should define boundaries that consist of a roughly square or rectangular area with a center line. Teams are then chosen. The number of balls being used is split between the two sides. An equal number of pins are set up along the back line of each side. Each team chooses and enters one side.

Object: To knock down all of the opponents' pins.

Play: A designated player signals the start of the game. From that point on, the playground balls are thrown at will towards the opposing team. Players, however, are never allowed to cross the middle line. If a player is struck by a ball thrown by an opponent, the player that was hit is temporarily out of the game. That player must walk off to the side of the playing field. Players may run anywhere on their side within the boundaries in order to dodge opponents' throws. A player is safe if the ball misses or strikes the ground before contact. A player may also catch a ball thrown by the other team. If a catch is made successfully, the thrower becomes out and the players that have been knocked out on the catcher's team get to reenter the game. If, at any time, a team is down to one player, that player cannot be eliminated by being hit, but may still catch the ball. This rule allows for there to be at least one player on each team to guard pins at all times.

The most important factor in the game is the pins. While the above is taking place, the real goal (since it is impossible to win by eliminating everyone), is to knock down all the opponents' pins. Once a pin is knocked over, it cannot be set up again! The game continues until one team knocks down all the opposing teams' pins. This team is the winner.

Personal comments: Dodgeball is a classic and famous for a reason, and this is a GREAT variation. If kids are not afraid to get hit by a ball and are competitive, this is a great game. It is a load of fun, and works on reflexes and coordination. This was one of my personal favorites and will catch on throughout the neighborhood. The pins make a fantastic extra challenge to an already exciting game!!

Broom Chaser[2]

Number of kids: 4 or more

Ages: any

Time allotted: 20 minutes or more

Space /Area: any decent sized safe area

Equipment: one broom

Description:

Startup: Players should define boundaries and choose and "It".

Object: To be the last player to become an It.

Play: The player who is chosen to be It begins with the broom. This person is called the "Broom Chaser". The Broom Chaser counts out loud to a certain number and the game begins. The Broom Chaser then tries to tag people with the bristled end of the broom. If a player is tagged, then that player becomes an It as well. These players do not switch places, but become a team. The original It still gets to hold the broom and does so at all times. The other Its help by grabbing and holding other players while yelling "Broom Chaser!" The Broom Chaser can then come and tag the person that is being held. This continues until all players but one have become an It by being tagged with the broom. The last non-It remaining is the winner and is the Broom Chaser in the next round.

Personal Comments: It sounds like plain tag with a broom, but it is much more. This game can be a lot of fun. Kids on the Broom Chaser's team will love ganging up to hold people. This allows everyone to stay active. It is also funny to watch the Broom Chaser flying at people wielding a broom. Go play this game and beware the broom!

Capture the Colors[3]

Number of kids: 2 teams of 4 or more

Ages: 8 and up

Time allotted: 30 minutes or more

Space /Area: any decent sized open area

Equipment: a makeshift "flag" for each player. Each team must have matching flags.

Description:

Startup: Players should choose two teams and define boundaries. Each team should select a captain. Everyone places the appropriate flag in the back of their waistline, so that it hangs out and may be grabbed.

Object: To get all of the other team's flags.

Play: Everyone scatters around the playing area and one player says "one, two, three, go" to signal the start of the game. The captains (and they only) try to capture the other team's flags. Everyone else simply tries to protect their own flag. If a player loses his or her flag, that player can help their captain by holding other players, so the captain may more easily grab their flags. The first team whose captain grabs all the other team's flags is the winner.

Personal Comments: This promotes team play, strategy, and individual skill. Make sure to rotate being captain, but both positions are enjoyable. Have fun teaming up on people to get their flag. Do not get too rough, but go out and have fun!

Capture the Flag

Number of kids: 2 teams of at least 3

Ages: 7 or older

Time allotted: 60 minutes or more

Space /Area: a large grassy or semi-wooded area, such as connecting backyards or a park or a field with some tress, etc.

Equipment: two makeshift flags

Description:

Startup: There are several variations to the rules. Depending on the number of players, each can be tried. The less players present, the simpler the game should be.
    Complex: Players are split evenly into attackers, middle men, and defenders.
    Medium: Players are split evenly into attackers and defenders.
    Simple: There are no set positions.

Object: To gain points by stealing the other team's flag.

Play: Rules vary slightly depending upon the level of complexity chosen, but the basic idea is consistent.
    Complex: In this version, the field is broken into three parts: two defense areas and a large area in the middle. Attackers and defender's split up into their own defense area. The middle men from both teams begin in the neutral area.
    Middle men are considered safe in the middle area and cannot be tagged. They may also never leave the middle area. The middle men's job is to tag attackers from the other team when they enter the middle area.
    Attackers may roam anywhere on the field. They are only safe in their own defense area and may be tagged anywhere else. Their job is to sneak past the middle men and then past other teams defense to try to steal the flag.
    Defenders may only protect their own flag and cannot leave their own defense area. Defenders are always safe and may never be tagged. Defenders only job is to tag the opponents' attackers when they enter the defense area.
    At any time an attacker may switch positions with a defender. Switches may only take place within one's defense area. Switches may only be done by changing one attacker for one defender, so there are a set number of attackers and defenders at all times. To avoid confusion middle men CANNOT switch positions with anyone.
    Skip to *Rules for all three*.
    Medium: In this version, there are no middle men. Only one middle line is used to divide the field in half. Defenders must stay in their own defense area, but attackers may go anywhere. Attackers may be tagged only after crossing the middle line into the other team's

defensive area. The number of defenders must remain constant on a side at all times, but a one for one switch with an attacker may be performed in the defense area.

Skip to *Rules for all three*.

Simple: There are no attackers and no defenders. In this version, only one middle line is used to divide the field in half. Any player is free to leave his or her side at any time, but that that player is vulnerable to being tagged upon crossing the middle line.

Now see *Rules for all three.*

Rules for all three: Before the game starts, a jail should be marked in one corner of each defense area. The flags should be planted anywhere in the defense area. As described above, once the game begins, players may be tagged by opponents when they enter the non-safe areas. Tagging is done literally when a defender or middle man tags an attacker. A tagged attacker must then throw up his or her hands to signal capture (faking this is not allowed!!). The captured player then goes to the other team's jail. If more than one player is in jail, they form a line with the first player caught in the front. A player in jail can be released if another attacker manages to get to the jail and tag him or her. Only the first player in line in the jail can be freed, so only one player can be freed at a time. If a player is freed, that player must again throw up his or her hands and must return to their own defensive area. Only then can the freed player once again attack.

Points are scored when an attacker manages to get a hold of the other team's flag. One point is scored for obtaining the flag then being tagged. Three points are scored for successfully returning to one's own defensive side with the flag before being tagged (for *complex*: one point is scored for obtaining the flag, two points for a return to the neutral territory, and three points are scored for a successful return to the other defensive side). Handing off the flag to another attacker is allowed! However, after the player holding the flag is caught, or if the flag touches the ground, everyone returns to their own side (even players in jail), points are awarded, the flag is returned, and play starts again.

Personal comments: All versions may sound complex and were difficult to describe, but this game is not at all complicated once you get going. Get everyone out on the field and try it. Tinker with the rules as necessary and you will easily get the hang of it. Once everyone understands the rules, this is an absolute blast! Kids can play this all day and night!! Parents can easily join in this game. This is really a childhood favorite of mine!

Variant: Jailbreak (also called Prisoner's Base[1]):

This is basically the same game, but all prisoners can be freed at the same time. The trick here is the attacker must put one or two feet in the jail and YELL "1, 2, 3, Jailbreak!" before being caught. This frees all of the players in the jail. The other trick is that there are no free walks back to one's own side. Once a player dashes free from jail, that player is free to be captured again, but is also free to capture the flag. This adds a little more intensity (as if it's needed!) and is a great time!!

Chain Tag

Number of kids: at least 5

Age: any

Time allotted: 20 minutes or more

Space /Area: a small open area

Equipment: none

Description:

Startup: Players should define relatively small boundaries and choose an "It".

Object: To be the last player tagged.

Play: Everyone spreads out inside the boundaries. The It counts out loud to a certain number and the game begins. The It then attempts to tag anyone and everyone. If a player is tagged, that player must join hands with the It. Those players then attempt to tag more people together. If either of the Its tags someone, that player must join hands with the person who tagged him or her. If the chain breaks at anytime, no tags are allowed until the chain is rejoined. The game continues until only one player is left untagged. This player is the winner and becomes the initial It for the next round.

Personal comments: The smaller the area the better. This makes it more difficult to avoid the chain of Its. Good for some laughs and excitement while getting good exercise!

Change Dodgeball[3]

Number of kids: 7 or more

Ages: 7 and up

Time allotted: 30 minutes or more

Space /Area: any decent sized open area

Equipment: one playground ball

Description:

Startup: One player is chosen to be "It" and everyone else gathers in a circle around him or her.

Object: To avoid being It.

Play: The It begins with the ball and throws it to another player (player 1). Player 1 throws the ball to another player (player 2). Player 2 throws the ball to another player (player 3). Player 3 throws the ball right back to the It. The trick to this game is the switch. As soon as player 2 throws the ball to player 3, players 1 and 2 must switch places in the circle. As soon as the It receives the ball from player 3, he or she tries to hit players 1 or 2 before they can get to their new location. If a player is hit during the switch, that player becomes It for the next round. If the It is unsuccessfully, he or she is It again. Passing to an adjacent person is never allowed! Play continues until players agree to quit.

Personal Comments: A good combination of ball tag and Dodgeball. Pretty high intensity and very exciting. Sounds simple and cheesy, but try this one out! The more players the better.

Chinese Tag

Number of kids: 3 or more

Ages: any

Time allotted: 20 minutes or more

Space /Area: any decent sized area

Equipment: none

Description:

Startup: Players should define boundaries and choose an "It".

Object: To avoid being It.

Play: Everyone spreads out in bounds. The It counts out loud to a certain number and the game begins. The It then tries to tag the other players. As in regular tag, if a tag is made, that person becomes the new It. The trick in this game is that the new It must keep one hand on the place where he or she was tagged (e.g. if tagged on the left shoulder, the new It must keep one hand on his or her left shoulder at all times until a tag is made). The next player tagged must do the same. The game continues until the players want to end.

Personal Comments: The best part of this game is to tag the other players in strange spots that are hard to hold. For example, if you tag someone on the knee, that player has the nearly impossible task of chasing other players while holding his or her knee. Watching the It can be the best part, especially if he was tagged in a funny place. It can be fun to be risky and run around near the It if he of she cannot move well. Diving at people's feet can be the most effective strategy in this game. Good for some laughs and some tough gaming!!

Circle Pass

Number of kids: 4 or more

Ages: any

Time allotted: 15 minutes or more

Space /Area: any open area

Equipment: none

Description:

Startup: A circle is marked or drawn in the playing area and players spread out on the edge of the circle in a random order.

Object: To be the last player remaining.

Play: One player says "Ready, Set, Go!" and the game begins. All players begin walking fast or running around the circle (players should choose before the game if running is allowed). The object is to eliminate players by passing them. If someone is passed, that player must step inside the circle and is eliminated until the next round. Players continue going around the circle, trying to pass each other, until only one is left. That player is the winner.

Personal Comments: Games don't get easier than this to play. Try changing directions, walking backwards, crawling, etc. or letting smaller or slower players run to try to even the odds. Great exercise, easy and fun to play!

Circle Survivor

Number of kids: at least 3

Ages: any

Time allotted: 15 minutes or more

Space /Area: a small grassy area

Equipment: one soccer ball for each child

Description:

Startup: Players should define strict boundaries within a small grassy area. Each player should take one soccer ball and enter the defined area.

Object: To be the last player with his or her ball inside the circle.

Play: Everyone counts to three and play begins. In this game, each player is responsible for his or her own ball. With no intentional physical contact, each player attempts to kick everyone else's ball out of the circle. If a player gets his or her ball kicked out of the circle, that player is eliminated from the game. When eliminated, the player must leave the circle. Play continues until everyone but one person has been eliminated. This player is the winner. Start another round!

Personal comments: This is high intensity. It's nerve-racking, but a must play. Try to be bold. Players should remember to protect their own ball, but keep trying to kick out other balls. Do not be scared and just stand still guarding your ball. Really be active, move around and try to get people out. The more offense you play, the more fun it is to win. Be aggressive and try this game!

Variant: Basketball Circle Survivor: In this game, basketballs are used instead of soccer balls. A circle should be drawn on cement as the playing area. The rest of the rules are the same.

Combination/Creative Tag

Number of kids: 3 or more

Ages: any

Time allotted: 20 minutes or more

Space /Area: any decent sized area

Equipment: depends on the rules chosen

Description:

Startup: Players should define boundaries and choose an "It". They should then decide on which rules to follow**. A combination can be done, such as Chinese-Reverse-Ball Tag, or players can form unique rules on their own.
**Throughout this book, several exciting versions of tag are described, but these are by no means every possibility. These can be used, as well as any other creative idea players imagine.

Object: To avoid being It.

Play: Everyone spreads out inside the boundaries. The It counts out loud to a certain number and the game begins. As in regular tag, if a tag is made, that player becomes the new It. Designated rules must be followed at all times. The game continues until the players agree to stop.

Personal Comments: Try this! Mix up different tag games to make them more original and challenging. Be creative! It can be fun to make the rules or just try a goofy combination of all the rules you know!!

Crack the Whip

Number of kids: at least 3

Ages: any

Time allotted: 15 minutes or more

Space /Area: a large grassy field or yard free of hard or rough ground

Equipment: none

Description:

Startup: A safe area must found to play. Players choose an order for everyone. The first player is deemed the leader and the other players are followers. Everyone gets in order and joins hands with the people next to them (forming "the whip"). The leader and the other end player may use two hands to hold on to the one person to whom they are connected.

Object: The leader's goal is to shake everyone off the whip. Everyone else must hold onto the whip as long as possible.

Play: Once everyone is ready, the leader begins to run and everyone else must keep up without breaking the chain. The leader should start to run around in a crazy fashion, bobbing, weaving, and turning. After everyone is running with full speed and making sharp turns, the players towards the back will begin to get sent flying off the whip because of the abrupt changes in movement. Slowly, everyone is tossed off the whip. Once most players have been thrown off the whip, mix up the order and play again. Try to play at least once from each position. The game really has no winner or end, but generally bragging rights go to the leader who shakes everyone off the fastest.

Personal Comments: You will get a little dirty playing this game, but that's all the fun. Wear protective clothing and play on a safe, soft, non-rocky field. Then go nuts. It is fun to be the leader and try to throw people and it is a blast to be at the end getting whipped around. Keep mixing up your positions and keep playing. See who can throw people off the fastest! It is fun to get jerked around and even to fly off and to watch others do so. Be as crazy as possible as the leader and hold on tight anywhere else!!

Dodgeball

Number of kids: 2 teams of at least 3

Ages: 7 and up

Time allotted: 40 minutes or more

Space /Area: a decent sized grass or black top area that can be split into two even sides

Equipment: playground balls (usually 2 or 3 depending upon the number of players)

Description:

Startup: Players should define boundaries. These should include a square or rectangular area with a middle line. Teams are chosen and split onto opposing sides of the middle line. The balls are all set on the middle line and each team stands on the back line of their half of the playing field.

Object: To have the last remaining player(s) in the game.

Play: Someone signals the start of the game. Players rush from the back line to get possession of the balls. The playground balls are then thrown at will towards the opposing team. Players are never to cross the middle line or go out of bounds. If a player is struck by a ball thrown by the other team, the struck player is temporarily out of the game and goes to sit on the side. Players may run anywhere within their half of the field in order to dodge the ball. A player is safe if a thrown ball misses or strikes the ground before contact. A player may also catch a ball thrown by the other team. If a catch is made successfully, the thrower becomes temporarily out, and everyone on the catcher's team that was temporarily out now rejoins the game. This continues until everyone on one side has been eliminated. The other team is the winner.

Personal comments: Dodgeball is a classic and famous for a reason. If kids are not afraid to get hit by a ball and are competitive, this is a great game. It is a load of fun, and works on reflexes and coordination. This was always one of my personal favorites and will catch on throughout the neighborhood!

Variant: Doctor Dodgeball: This game uses the same set of rules with two changes. The first change is that players sit down instead of leaving the field when they are hit. The second change is that one player from each team is designated as a doctor before the game. The doctor can bring a player back into the game by touching him or her. The doctors can stand safely on the sidelines and may enter the playing field at will. Once the doctors enter the playing field, they may be eliminated like any other player. Once a doctor is eliminated, he or she is out of the game for good, and the game finishes in the same fashion.

Variant: Free For All Dodgeball: In this game, every player tries to eliminate each other. There is no middle line. All other rules apply. Catching the ball only results in the thrower being eliminated. The last player left wins.

Variant: Alley Dodgeball[3]: Divide into 3 teams. Split the playing field into three sections, instead of in halves. In this version, two teams split into the outside areas and one team gets into the inside area. The outside teams are trying to hit the inside players with the balls. If a player is hit, that player is out and there is no reentry. Catches can be made and the catcher is safe. If a player in the middle grabs a ball at any time, that player should toss it back to an outside player. The last player still alive in the middle wins. Take turns with which team gets to be on the inside.

Variant: Square Dodgeball[3]: A square is formed for boundaries. One team must stay inside the square; the other must stay outside at ALL times. Players on the outside are on full time offense and inside players are full time defense. If an inside player is hit, the outside team earns 2 points. If a ball is caught, it does not score points. Balls that land or are caught inside must immediately be returned to the outside. Intentional failure to return a ball results in the outside team earning a point. One point is also awarded if an inside player crosses accidentally or purposefully to the outside of the square. After 2 minutes, the teams switch. Two or three rounds are played and the team with the highest score total wins.

Flashlight Tag

Number of kids: at least 3

Ages: any

Time allotted: at least 45 minutes

Space /Area: a large field with hiding places or several connecting yards in a neighborhood

Equipment: one flashlight for each "It" (usually just 1, but can be 2 with many players)

Description:

Startup: Players determine an area in which to play. Players then choose a base to tag or a line to cross to be "safe". Lastly, the "It" is chosen.

Object: To return safely to base without being revealed by the flashlight.

Play: Everyone begins at the base or safe line. The It waits there for at least one minute while the rest of the players run and hide within the determined area. After that time, the Its job is to find the hiders and to shine the flashlight on them. While the It is doing this, the attempt to sneak back to base or across the safe line without the It noticing them and spotting them with the flashlight. If a hider is successful at reaching the base, the hider announces it loudly and play continues. Play continues until each It catches someone who will replace them during the next round. If all hiders become safe, the last hider to come in will be It for the next round.

Personal Comments: Make sure that the playing area is large with many places to hide. Do not allow the It to simply guard the base. This game is more fun with a larger space, so the It has to go out looking, which creates more chances for people to break for base. Flashlights can work from far away, so the It can wander and still nail someone. It is not fun for the hiders if the It just sits next to the base. As the It, do not get carried away and wander too far off, but give the hiders a good chance. It is also more fun when the hiders are not too conservative and do not remain hidden where the It has no chance to spot them. It is the hiders' job to be risky and break for base. This is a lot of fun and excitement and is highly suggested for a good night time or camping game.

Frisbee~TM~ War

Number of kids: 3 or more

Ages: any

Time allotted: 15 minutes or more

Space /Area: any decent sized yard or field

Equipment: one Frisbee for each player

Description:

Startup: Players define loose boundaries and each chooses a Frisbee.

Object: To be the last person remaining that has an unflipped Frisbee.

Play: Play begins with all players throwing their Frisbees. At first players may want to throw conservatively to ensure that their Frisbee does not land up side down. Eventually (if skill allows), each player should start throwing their Frisbees at each other's in order to knock an opponent's Frisbee over onto its back. This is the way to eliminate players. If a player's Frisbee lands up side down, by any means, that player is eliminated. One exception is that no one can physically touch an opponent's Frisbee in any way. A player can only hit an opponents Frisbee by *throwing* their own. A player may catch his or her own Frisbee in midair or if it is rolling on its side, but if it comes to rest and is up side down, that player is eliminated and must sit out until next game. The winner is the last person remaining. After a winner is found, a new game may start. Single games or a series can be played.

Personal Comments: A good mix of defense and offense is key. It is good to throw conservatively, but is also fun to fling your Frisbee toward an opponent's. So go be a little risky and have fun! This game is really a blast once you get good at tossing and controlling your Frisbee. It will probably seem hard at first, but gets more and more entertaining with skill and experience.

Interference Tag[3]

Number of kids: 4 or more

Age: any

Time allotted: 20 minutes or more

Space /Area: any decent sized open area

Equipment: none

Description:

Startup: Players should define boundaries. They then choose one player to be the "Runner" and one to be the "Chaser".

Object: To avoid being the Chaser.

Play: Everyone spreads out inside the boundaries. The Runner counts out loud to a certain number and the game begins. The Chaser then tries to tag the Runner. If successful, the Runner becomes the Chaser, and the former Chaser instantly calls out another player's name. The person called instantly becomes the new Runner and play continues. The trick to this game is that at any time, another player may run "interference" on the chase. This is accomplished by tagging the Runner and yelling "Interference!" The "interfering" player instantly becomes the new Runner until tagged or until someone else performs an interference. The game ends when all players agree to stop.

Personal comments: This is a game that may seem atypical, but is a load of fun. It can be played with just a few, but more kids add more interfering and confusion which adds to the fun. Go out and try it, it is a great game!

Jack, Jack, Show Your Light[4]

Number of kids: 4 or more

Ages: 8 and up

Time allotted: 1 hour or more

Space /Area: a large semi-wooded area

Equipment: one flashlight, one watch, and one whistle

Description:

Startup: Play is best when it is dark or becoming dark outside. Players should strictly define boundaries. One player is chosen to be "Jack". Jack gets the flashlight and the whistle.

Object: To catch Jack.

Play: Play begins by giving Jack getting a 50 second head start into the woods. After this count, all other players scatter to look for Jack. Once the chase begins, Jack is required to show his of her flashlight every 30 seconds by turning it on, holding it straight out, and spinning in a circle. Players should yell "Jack, Jack, Show Your Light" to inspire Jack to show the flashlight. When a player is able to see Jack's light, that player must yell "Run, Jack, Run" to give Jack fair notice. If no one can see the light, no one will yell "Run, Jack, Run". If this happens, Jack must stop and blow his whistle and swing his light continuously until someone spots the light and yells "Run, Jack, Run". The game ends when someone catches Jack. If no one catches him after 30 minutes, Jack must stay still, blow his whistle, and leave his light on until someone finds him. Whoever catches Jack first is Jack for the next round.

Personal Comments: This is really an exciting game. This game keeps everyone moving and excited. It can be scary, exciting, and fun at the same time. Kids will get hooked on this game. The key is finding a good safe area to play. Try to do so because this game will be a hit!!

Jump Rope

Number of kids: 1 or more

Ages: any

Time allotted: 20 minutes or more

Space /Area: an open paved area

Equipment: one or two jump ropes (slightly heavy ropes can be substituted)

Description:

Startup: If there are 3 or more players, two rope spinners and one or more jumpers must be chosen. Then players should find a good open area to play.

Object: To continually jump the rope(s).

Play: For only one person, the game is simple. The player simply takes one end of the rope in each hand and rotates it over his or her body so the rope passes underfoot as the player jumps. Once a player gets good, he or she can add challenges such as hopping on one foot, turning the rope underfoot twice on one jump, crossing arms, trying to bounce a small ball, or creating new tricks.

For three or more players, Double Dutch can be played. Two ropes are needed. The two spinners each take one end of each rope in a different hand. They must spin one rope in one direction and the second rope in the opposing direction. The jumper(s) then jump into the middle and must continually jump both of the ropes. Some of the same tricks may be done in this game as well, plus players can create many more. Players can take turns by jumping in and out of the ropes or play can continue until a player is hit by one of the ropes. Spinners and jumpers should switch positions every few minutes so everyone can jump.

Option: Spinners can chant their favorite rhymes while spinning.

Personal comments: This is great exercise! It is also fun to be creative and try new tricks. The more you practice, the better you will get. Mastering new tricks is exciting, but even basic jumping can be a lot of fun.

Keep Away Chase

Number of kids: 3 or more, or teams of 2 or more

Ages: any

Time allotted: 15 minutes or more

Space /Area: a large area with obstacles, such as a playground or adjacent yards

Equipment: one object to hold

Description:

Startup: One object is chosen with which a player can easily run. One person or team is then picked to start with the object. Everyone else become chasers.

Object: To possess the object as much as possible.

Play: Everyone gives the object holder(s) a 30 second head start and then the game begins. The chasers must catch whoever has the object and tag them (or put both arms around them, whichever rule is decided). If a holder is caught, the object must be given to that chaser. Time must be allowed for the new object holder to escape, and then the game continues. If teams are used, the object may be passed from teammate to teammate until someone is caught. The game continues until the players decide to stop.

Personal Comments: This is a good tag/keep away combination. It's a ton of exercise and a load of fun. Go play this one!! A couple girls to whom I taught tennis used to steal my hat and run around a playground with it until I caught them. It's a blast! That's how this game basically invented itself. –thank you Danielle and Ali.

King (or Queen) of the Hill

Number of kids: at least 3

Ages: 10 and up

Time allotted: 20 minutes or more

Space /Area: usually a grassy hill (but creativity can be used)

Equipment: none

Description:

Startup: Finding a good safe hill is the most challenging part. Anything else that a player can be atop and pulled down or away from safely will work. A King or Queen is chosen and proceeds to the top of the "hill". The rest of the players remain at the bottom.

Object: To become the King or Queen on top of the hill and stay there for as long as possible.

Play: The chosen King or Queen signals the start of the game. The rest of the players then try to climb the hill and pull off the King or Queen. When a King or Queen is pulled off, everyone tries to take his or her place at the top. The struggle from then on is constant, with players always trying to get to the top and stay there. This game can last for a certain length of time, and whoever is on top after that time is the winner. It may also simply be continuous until the players are too tired to persist.

Personal comments: This game can get a little rough, but if kids are responsible, it can be a lot of fun. Do not play if you do not enjoy physical activities and contact. This game allows children to gain some strength and stamina, while enjoying good fun and competition. This is good for kids who like physical activity and do not mind getting a little dirty.

Kings and Queens[2]

Number of kids: 4 or more

Ages: any

Time allotted: 30 minutes or more

Space /Area: any decent sized safe area

Equipment: one soft ball

Description:

Startup: Players should define boundaries and choose an "It".

Object: To be the last player to become an It.

Play: The It begins with the ball. Everyone spreads out in bounds. The It counts out loud to a certain number and the game begins. Similar to ball tag, the It attempts to hit other players with the ball. Players in this game must keep closed fists and are allowed to touch or block the ball with their fists. If a player is hit on any part of their body except the fist, he or she also becomes an It. This player does not switch places with the It, but they become a team. The Its can all pick up the ball with their bare hands, run with it, and toss it to each other in order to hit other players and make more players It. If given the chance, non-Its may also hit or carry the ball with their fists, but the ball may never touch any other part of the body and the non-Its hands may never unfist. This way non-Its can try to keep the ball out of the hands of the Its. The game continues until all players but one have become Its. The last player remaining is the King or Queen and is the first It in the next round.

Personal Comments: This game is a blast and is a great for a lot of laughs. It is quite a good spin-off of ball tag. Being It and non-It are both very exciting in this game. The element of passing between Its with the non-Its able to block and carry the ball is too much fun to pass up. This takes some strategy, teamwork, and practice. Get kids playing this game and they will love it!!

Mini-Tennis

Number of kids: 2, or 2 teams of 2

Ages: any

Time allotted: 30 minutes or more

Space /Area: a tennis court (or see variants)

Equipment: a tennis ball and one racquet for each player (or see variants)

Description:

Startup: Players get on opposing sides of the net, each standing in one opposing service box (or use both service boxes for team play). The service boxes are the boundaries for this game. Choose one player or team to serve first.

Object: To score 15 points first.

Play: Each point begins with a serve. Serves are simple bumps over the net into the opponent's box. After the ball lands, the returner then bumps it back to the server. A point is then played similar to tennis (the ball must land in bounds and can bounce a maximum of one time). The ball can never be hit hard; instead placement and finesse must be used. Players may run anywhere on their side of the net and may hit the ball in the air or after one bounce. A player wins the point when his or her opponent misses the ball and it bounces twice or the opponent hits the ball into the net or out of bounds. Each point won is worth 1 point. Like ping-pong, each player takes turn serving 5 times. The winner is the first player to score 15 points (must win by two).

Personal Comments: This game is addicting! It takes a lot of practice to get good, but try lobs and drop shots. Use placement and strategy. The better you become, the more fun it is. Tons of fun and more exercise than you would possibly imagine!

Variants: If no tennis court is available, people can play with two boxes on a driveway or drawn on a street, etc. Players can also have a gap between the boxes or have them touching. A makeshift net can be made if desired. Hands can also be used instead of racquets.

Mulberry Bush

Number of kids: at least 2

Ages: any

Time allotted: 10 minutes or more

Space /Area: any small open area

Equipment: none

Description:

Startup: Everyone forms a circle. Players may circle around an object (such as a bush) if desired.

Object: To enjoy the game.

Play: Players began to skip around in a circle while chanting. The first lyrics chanted are: "Here we go 'round the mulberry bush, the mulberry bush, the mulberry bush, here we go 'round the mulberry bush, so early in the morning". Players continue to skip around the circle while singing the next verses. The succeeding verses are based around a daily activity. One example is: "This is the way we brush our teeth, brush our teeth, brush our teeth, this is the way we brush our teeth, so early in the morning". Any activity may be substituted for "brush our teeth". Players should take turns naming the activity to sing. Other common verses are: wash our clothes, iron our clothes, sweep the floor, eat our food, and get dressed up, but anything can be used. Players should also act out the action while skipping and singing. For example, while singing the "brush our teeth" verse, players should pretend to be brushing their teeth while they skip and sing.

Personal comments: An enjoyable, easy game, that little children and anyone else can play. A true classic that is good, clean fun.

Nutmeg

Number of kids: at least 3

Ages: any

Time allotted: 20 minutes or more

Space /Area: a small grassy area

Equipment: one soccer ball for each child

Description:

Startup: Players should set strict boundaries within a small grassy area. Each player takes one soccer ball and enters the defined area.

Object: To be the last player remaining.

Play: One person counts to three and play begins. Player's then attempt to kick any ball through another player's legs. A player does not have to keep the ball with which he or she began. Players may use or steal others' balls as well as their own. Hands are never allowed to be used. No pushing, holding, or kicking is allowed, but a player can do anything else to kick any ball through another's legs. If a player has a ball kicked through his or her legs, that player is eliminated and must step out of bounds. If a ball goes out of bounds, the people who have been eliminated put it back into play, or a short time out is called to retrieve it. Play continues until everyone but one person has been eliminated. That player is the winner. Start another round!

Personal comments: This is high intensity. It's nerve-racking, but a must play. Try to be bold. Players should protect their own legs, but be sure to attack others' as well. Do not be timid and just stand with your legs together. Really be active, move around and try to get people out. The more offense you play, the more fun it is to win. Give this game a shot!

Obstacle Course

Number of kids: 1 or more

Ages: any

Time allotted: at least 30 minutes

Space /Area: anywhere where children have, or can build, obstacles to safely move over, through, and around

Equipment: anything safe

Description:

Startup: Setting up the course is a fun part of this game. Players should invent their own obstacle course. They can use pre-existing objects (trees, etc.) or they can place or build their own. Find a good area and be creative.

Object: To finish the obstacle course, or to do it the fastest.

Play: Once the obstacle course is created, each player should take turns attempting to complete it. If desired, players can time each other to see who can finish the fastest. One player can conquer a course alone just for the challenge, as well.

Personal Comments: This process seems very simple, but can be as complex as you would like. Actually, the more complex the course, the more fun. Try to build or come up with difficult and challenging obstacles. Most of the fun is being creative with the set-up. See who can come up with the craziest course, then go for it!!!

Races

Number of kids: 2 or more

Ages: any

Time allotted: 15 minutes or more

Space /Area: anywhere safe

Equipment: usually none, but depends on the race decided

Description:

Startup: Players should decide on the type of race desired and determine a start and finish line.

Object: To finish the race first or the fastest.

Play: There is a plethora of racing possibilities because almost anything can be a race. Some common races are having teams of two and racing in a wheel barrow position, or having a leap frog race, or racing bikes, or racing around houses, etc. These can all be a blast and provide entertainment for many kids, but any type of race may be performed. Players can race one at a time and try to make the best time, or they can race against each other at the same time to see who can finish first.

Personal Comments: Be creative and make up all sorts of races. Any crazy body position or team challenge can be used. Have the winner(s) pick the next type of race. Be competitive, but have fun and try to create some races that anybody might win.

Reverse Tag

Number of kids: 3 or more

Ages: any

Time allotted: 20 minutes or more

Space /Area: any decent sized area

Equipment: none

Description:

Startup: Players should define boundaries and choose an "It".

Object: To avoid being It.

Play: Everyone spreads out in bounds. The It counts out loud to a certain number and the game begins. As in regular tag, if a tag is made, the tagged player becomes the new It. The trick in this game is that everyone must run backwards at all times, even the It. The game continues until the players agree they want to stop.

Personal Comments: This is a good way to work on your backwards running! There are a lot of falls in this game, which can be extremely funny. This game is good for an all around good time.

Scorpion Tag

Number of kids: at least 3

Ages: any

Time allotted: 20 minutes or more

Space /Area: a small grassy area

Equipment: none

Description:

Startup: Players should define strict boundaries (usually small to even the odds). An "It" is then chosen to be the "Scorpion".

Object: To avoid being It.

Play: The Scorpion gets into a position like a Scorpion (walking belly up on hands and feet). The other players spread out in bounds. The Scorpion then counts out loud to a certain number and the game begins. The Scorpion then tries to tag other players, but must stay in the correct position at all times. A tag is made by touching another player with a raised leg (like a Scorpion stinging). If tagged, that player is the new Scorpion and the game continues. The game ends when the players agree to stop.

Personal Comments: This is a fun game for just goofing off. Enjoy taunting the Scorpion by running close by and dodging the sting. Do not play too seriously and do not worry about becoming It. Being the Scorpion is challenging, but lots of fun. Make sure the playing area is small enough that the Scorpion has a good chance. Go enjoy this game!

Skrag

Number of kids: 3 or more

Ages: 10 or older

Time allotted: at least 20 minutes

Space /Area: a large grassy field or yard free of hard or rough ground

Equipment: a soft football

Description:

Startup: Players should select a ball and define boundaries. One player starts with the ball.

Object: There are two. The man with the ball must stay on his or her feet and avoid everyone else. Everyone else's goal is to tackle the player with the ball.

Play: Play begins with everyone getting into a circle. Whoever has the ball throws it up into the air. Whichever player feels bold enough grabs the ball and runs. Every other player then tries to tackle whoever grabbed the ball, for as long as it takes to do so. Once tackled, the tackled player throws the football back up into the air. Another player then grabs it, and play continues as before. The ball is not allowed to be passed or fumbled. If fumbled, the player who dropped it should immediately retrieve the ball or be tackled anyway. The game ends when everyone is too tired to continue.

Personal comments: Make sure everyone gets the ball! The trick to having fun in this game is not backing down. It is more fun if everyone gets a turn with the ball and no two kids hog it. This game does get rough, but that is the whole point. Do not play if you are afraid of being tackled. Skrag lets out a little aggression and is actually a ton of exercise. Play safe, but go out and play hard. This game is a blast!

Small Hockey

Number of kids: 2 teams of at least 2

Ages: 8 and up

Time allotted: 45 minutes or more

Space /Area: the end of a culdesac is optimal, but any blacktop or concrete area will do if it is safe and can have equal goals placed on each side

Equipment: one hockey stick for each child, at least one rubber street hockey ball, two goals (can be makeshift or bought), roller blades optional (but fun)…and any appropriate safety equipment

Description:

Startup: A field of play is chosen by the players, goals are set at each end, and teams are decided. The ball is set in the middle.

Object: To out score the other team.

Play: One player from each team faces off to begin the game. This is done by having one player from each team slap their sticks together three times above the ball, then trying to take possession of it. This game rules are similar to regular hockey without the checking and rough play. Passing and dribbling the ball with the stick are legal (using hands is not, except for the goalie). One player usually plays goalie, and the rest split up into offenders and defenders. Everyone then attempts to score. If a goal is made, the scoring team get one point and another face off ensues. If the ball goes out of bounds, the team who did not knock it out gains possession. Teams can play timed periods or until a certain score is reached.

Personal comments: This game is fantastic! I spent many an after school afternoon playing this with friends. It can satisfy every kid for an entire afternoon. It is great exercise, teaches team lessons, and develops a lot of good sports skills. Once kids get into it, they will want to play this for a long time. It takes time to get good, but getting better and better makes the games more and more exciting. Kids will come back thrilled from an experience with this game.

Variant: Roller Hockey: The rules are the same except everyone but the goalies wears roller blades.

Variant: Broom Hockey: The rules are also the same except brooms are used instead of sticks and a larger ball must be used (such as a playground ball). Also, play is usually on grass for this variant.

Small Soccer

Number of kids: 2 teams of at least 2

Ages: any

Time allotted: at least 30 or 40 minutes

Space /Area: a good sized yard or field

Equipment: one soccer ball and makeshift goals

Description:

Startup: A field of play is chosen by the players and small goals are set up. Goals can be anything from two posts on a fence to two cones set on the ground. Teams are picked. A coin flip or "rock, paper, scissors" is used to decide who starts with the ball.

Object: To out score the other team.

Play: Rules of regular soccer basically apply, but these rules are not as strict (for example, off sides is usually not considered a penalty in small soccer). Teams should have defenders and offenders, but these players may go anywhere on the field. There is usually no goalie because of the small goals and field. This is a simple game of dribbling, passing, and scoring in small goals. One team starts with the ball at their goal line and brings it up the field. Each team then tries to control the ball and score through the other team's goal. When a team is scored on, they begin with possession at their goal line and play resumes. Teams can play timed periods or play until a certain score is reached.

Personal comments: Another fun mini-sport that is good for entire afternoons. It is also great exercise, teaches team lessons, and develops coordination and stamina. Mini soccer can be a goof off game as well as serious competition, and anyone can play!

Tail-Grabbers

Number of kids: at least 7

Age: any

Time allotted: 25 minutes or more

Space /Area: a good sized open area

Equipment: a makeshift tail for every two or three children

Description:

Startup: Players should define boundaries. Choose one or more tail-grabbers (depending on the number of players). Everyone else splits into even groups of two or three. Each group gets into a line, holding the hips of the person in front of them. The player in the back of each line wears the tail for his or her team. This is done by tucking the tail into the waistline, so that it is hanging out.

Object: To be the last team with their tail.

Play: Everyone gets inside the boundaries. The tail-grabber(s) says "Go" and the game begins. The tail-grabber then attempts to pull the tail off each team. If a team loses their tail, they are out of the game. A team can lose their tail if a tail-grabber pulls it off, or if a player breaks the chain by releasing the hips of the player in front of them. The last team with their tail is the winner. One of the winners gets to be the tail-grabber for the next round.

Personal comments: This is a different type of game which makes it a lot of fun. This game can be played with as little as seven, but it takes many kids to reach its full potential, so go out and try to get kids to play, it will be worth it!

Thirty-Two Tips

Number of kids: at least 2

Ages: 7 and up

Time allotted: 30 minutes or more

Space/Area: any area with a basketball hoop

Equipment: one basketball

Description:

Startup: Choose the area to play and decide which player gets the ball first. Choosing the first player can be done with a shoot out at the free throw line.

Object: To be the first to score thirty-two points.

Play: The player with the ball "checks" it and the game begins. Checking is done by passing the ball to another player and he or she passes it back. Each players is then trying to score thirty-two points. Using basic basketball rules, if any player makes a basket, that player gets the ball back and the game continues. Fouls and two and three pointers apply, as in regular basketball. If a player misses a basket, two things can happen. Any other player may then grab the ball and score. If a player is able to tip the ball in, the player who tipped the ball gets the basket, and the player who shot the original shot has his or her score erased to zero. Tipping the ball requires a player to catch the rebound and shoot it back in while being in midair. This process continues until one player reaches thirty-two points, and this player is the winner.

Personal Comments: This game is non-stop excitement! Great for basketball skills and fun, competitive exercise. Even if you are not that great at basketball, this game is great to try! As you get better at tipping, this game becomes even more fun. The best part is seeing what kind of crazy tip ins you can pull off. Really be aggressive and try to reset people's scores! But be careful to protect your points at the same time.

Three Court Soccer[3]

Number of kids: 2 teams of 4 or more

Ages: any

Time allotted: 45 minutes or more

Space /Area: a good sized open grassy field

Equipment: one or two soccer balls (players' choice)

Description:

Startup: Players should define boundaries. Boundaries need to a large rectangular area broken up into 5 sections. There should be one large section in the middle and a slightly smaller end zone on each end. There also needs to be a small strip (about 5 or 10 feet) of neutral area in between the central area and each end zone. Choose teams. One team gets into the middle and the other team splits evenly between the end zones. The team in the end zones is the offense.

Object: To score the most points.

Play: One player on the offense starts with the ball on the outside edge of one end zone. That player passes the ball to one of his teammates in that box and the point begins. If two balls are used, one ball should start at each end. Once the ball is passed in bounds, the offense must then attempt to pass the ball across the middle area to a teammate in the other end zone. The ball must be passed along the ground. The defense is allowed to stop these balls by any means necessary without leaving their middle area. The offense also cannot leave their designated area. If a pass goes through the middle area and through the other end zone, or if it is stopped by the defense, the ball is dead. The ball is then returned to the offense, again is set on the back of the end zone and passed in bounds. If the offense successfully passes the ball through the middle to another player in the other end zone, they score one point. Another point then immediately starts by setting it on the end zone line and passing it in bounds. After five minutes, the teams switch. Each team gets two rounds as offense. Whoever has the most points at the end wins.

Personal Comments: A high paced, fun version of Small Soccer. This takes good team work and good offensive and defensive skill. Good for improving soccer skills or to just go play and have fun!

Touch Football

Number of kids: 2 teams of 2 or more

Ages: any

Time allotted: 45 minutes or more

Space /Area: a good sized open grassy field

Equipment: one football

Description:

Startup: Players should define boundaries. Boundaries need to a large rectangular area with an end zone on each end. Choose teams. One team is chosen to kick off and each team goes to opposite sides of the field.

Object: To score the most points.

Play: One team "kicks off" to the other by kicking, punting, or throwing the ball. The other team then tries to run the ball towards the other end zone. This team is the offense. The offensive player with the ball is "down" when he or she is touched with two hands by any defensive player. Following basic football rules, teams then attempt to score touch downs back and forth. The offense gets four downs to get a first down. They may run or pass. On fourth down, the offense may punt the ball to the other team if they choose. On offense, usually only one player is a quarterback and the rest are recievers. Quarterbacks should not be allowed to run the ball every play. Instead, teams should decide how often they can run, such as once every four downs. First downs can be made by going approximately ten yards or by completing two passes; players decide. On defense, players should attempt to stop the offense by covering the recievers and quarterback. Defensive players cannot hold players and must count aloud to ten before they can run and try to tag the quarterback. If an offense is able reach the end zone successfully, they receive one point. This team must then kick off to the other team. The first team to reach a given number of points, usually five, is the winner. Teams may also play for a certain length of time, such as twenty minutes halves, and whoever has the most points is the winner.

Personal Comments: A true classic that every child should know. This can provide entertainment for hours. It is great exercise that can inspire interest in an organized sport. If you have or have not played this before, get out and there and try it. This is a great game!

Variant: One Chance Football: In this game, the same rules apply accept the offense gets limited downs to score and a much smaller field must be used. One variant can be that offenses get no first downs, so they only have four chances to score. Another variant can be that each team only gets one down to score. This must be done on a field that is only about ten yards long. Players take turns trying to go the whole ten yards.

Ultimate Frisbee™

Number of kids: 2 teams of 3 or more

Ages: 8 and up

Time allotted: 45 minutes or more

Space /Area: a large grassy field

Equipment: One Frisbee

Description:

Startup: Players should define a large field with designated side lines and goal lines. Teams are then decided.

Object: To score the most points by making touchdowns.

Play: Teams begin on opposite sides of the field. One team begins by "throwing off" to the other team. This is done when one teams throws the Frisbee down the field towards the other team. The receiving team catches or picks up the Frisbee and the game begins. The team with the Frisbee is now on offense. They must advance the Frisbee up the field by throwing it to one another. Once a player has possession of the Frisbee, that player is not allowed to move with it. He or she can only throw the Frisbee to another player. To score, teams must advance the Frisbee all the way across their goal line. The defensive team is always trying to take possession of the Frisbee. Intentional contact is not allowed, but anything else really goes. The defenders may guard the other players and try to intercept the Frisbee in the air. If the defenders gain possession of it, they become the offense and attempt to advance in the opposite direction. If the Frisbee should hit the ground at any time, the defending team takes possession. If any team crosses the goal line successfully, they score a touchdown and get one point. As in football, the teams return to their sides and the team who scored "throws off" the Frisbee and the game continues. The game can be played by quarters or halves and whoever scores the most touch downs wins. The game may also end when a certain score is reached.

Personal Comments: This game is quickly becoming more and more popular and for good reason. It is fantastic exercise and an excellent game. It takes skill, coordination, and endurance. Ultimate Frisbee also takes a lot of practice. Do not be frustrated at first. Practice tossing the Frisbee between games and play until you get good. The more you play, the better it gets!!

Variant: Boundary Ball[3]: Rules are basically the same except a chosen ball is passed in lue of the Frisbee. Also, a score is made by *rolling* the ball across the goal line (must be on the ground!). For this, smaller goals must be setup with cones in the middle of the goal lines. If the roll is unsuccessful, the defending team automatically takes possession.

Water Fights

Number of kids: at least 2

Ages: any

Time allotted: 30 minutes or more

Space /Area: a yard, front and back, or grassy outdoor area with water or hose access

Equipment: be creative (examples: water guns, buckets, water balloons, cups, hoses)

Description:

Startup: Each player should gather all the supplies they desire before the game and prepare them as necessary. Enough supplies should be gathered to enable the game to last awhile (but breaks can be taken to get more stuff and to refill, of course). Boundaries can be set if desired. Teams are chosen or a free-for-all is decided.

Object: To get the other people as wet as possible and to just have fun.

Play: Really no rules apply, except there is no rough housing or physical play. Each kid uses their supplies any way they see fit to soak the other people or team(s). Reloading with more water is always acceptable. Play ends whenever the players decide to stop.

Personal comments: Great for a hot day or just to take out extra energy in a positive way. The more stuff you can use, the better. Be creative, get some buckets and anything else that could be good to launch water and go out and have fun!

You're Under Arrest!

Number of kids: 3 or more

Ages: 8 and up

Time allotted: at least 1 hour

Space /Area: a large, safe neighborhood or biking area

Equipment: one bike for each child and any necessary safety equipment for biking

Description:

Startup: Players should define large boundaries, roughly the size of a neighborhood. A base is also chosen as the jail. One person is chosen to be the criminal (or 2 if there are many players). Everyone else is police.

Object: To catch the criminals and bring them back to jail.

Play: Everyone begins at the jail. Once a criminal(s) is chosen, the criminal is allowed a two to three minute head start on his or her bike into the playing area. The police then split up and ride out to find the criminal. To capture a criminal, the police must ride up next to him or her and say "You're under arrest!" Tagging is NOT permitted because a player could knock someone off their bike and cause serious injury! If arrested, the criminal must ride to base with the police officer. The game ends when each criminal is caught.

It is important for the police to check back to base every few minutes to see if the criminals have been caught. This prevents players from riding around looking for criminals when there are none left. It also ensures the next round will begin as soon as possible. Whichever police officer caught the criminal is then the next criminal.

Personal Comments: This is best for older kids, but anyone who can safely rides bikes can participate. Use as big of an area as possible, without getting out of hand. This allows for the criminals to "hide out" a little more. The longer the hunt, the more rewarding the catch is. This is great exercise too! Roam the neighborhood and play this game all afternoon!

Activity Level IV

Base Rush[3]

Number of kids: at least 4

Ages: any

Time allotted: 20 minutes or more

Space /Area: a long, open strip of grassy land

Equipment: several identical objects that can serve as bases (Frisbees, etc.) -one less than the number of children playing is needed (e.g. 7 bases are needed for 8 players).

Description:

Startup: Players should choose a long field with a defined starting line and ending line. The bases are then set up along the ending line. There should be one less base set up than there are kids playing.

Object: To be the last player remaining.

Play: Everyone lines up at the starting line. One player says "Ready, Set, Go!" and everyone races for the end line. A player then becomes safe by getting to and standing on one of the bases. No fighting for the bases is allowed; the first player there gets to stay on the base. Only one player can safely land on each base. This way one player will not find a base and is eliminated. One base is then removed and another round begins. This continues until there is only one player left, who is the winner.

Personal Comments: A good game of speed, but some strategy is also involved, in which base to go for, etc. It is like musical chairs with a whole lot more running. Good exercise, good competition, and clean fun!

British Bulldog

Number of kids: at least 4

Ages: 8 and up

Time allotted: 30 minutes or more

Space /Area: a good sized yard or field

Equipment: none

Description:

Startup: Players should choose two lines for boundaries, about thirty or forty feet apart, and designate sidelines that cannot be crossed. Players should also choose one player to be the "Bulldog". All players then line up on one side of the designated field. The Bulldog begins in the middle of the two lines.

Object: To be the last person captured by the Bulldogs.

Play: The game begins when the Bulldog yells "British Bulldog!". Everyone must then attempt to cross the field to the other designated line, without ever going out of bounds. While players cross, the Bulldog tries to capture people and make them Bulldogs also. The Bulldog accomplishes this by lifting someone in the air while yelling "one, two, three, British Bulldog!". If this is completed successfully, the lifted person then becomes a Bulldog along with the other Bulldog(s). Everyone who was safe lines up again and when everyone is ready, the Bulldogs again yell "British Bulldog!", and the process repeats. This continues until only one person is left uncaptured. This player is then the winner and the initial Bulldog for the next round.

Personal comments: It really helps to gang up on people. Some people definitely may take more than one person to lift. Get the smaller players first, then go for the bigger ones. Do not play if you are afraid of a little physical play. Sometimes this game can get a little rough, but that makes it fun! Be safe, but prepared to be tough and have some high intensity action!

Category Tag (also called Sit-down Tag)

Number of kids: at least 3

Ages: any

Time allotted: 20 minutes or more

Space /Area: a small grassy area

Equipment: none

Description:

Startup: Players should define small boundaries and choose an "It". A category for play is then chosen by the It and announced to all (examples: funny movies, actors, basketball players, candy bars, etc.).

Object: To avoid becoming It.

Play: Everyone spreads out in bounds. The It counts out loud to a certain number and the game begins. The It then attempts to tag everyone. The twist on this game is the category. A player may sit down safely until the It moves away if he or she is able to call out a member of the defined category. (Example: if the category is basketball players, a player about to get tagged may yell "Michael Jordan" and sit before he or she is tagged.) To be safe, the word must be yelled AND the player must be on the ground before being tagged. Players may not sit down until they have successfully called the name. If a player successfully sits, the It must chase someone else and the seated player must stand as quickly as possible. Once a word is said, such as "Michael Jordan", no other player can use it. This is why the words must be yelled, so that all can hear. Once a player is tagged once, twice, or three times (decided at the beginning), that player becomes It, decides on a new category, and the game begins again.

Option: Running can be allowed in a small area, or no moving at all can be decided.

Personal comments: The It must be sure to run fast, the faster the It runs, the less time the others have to think. This seems cheesy, but it is a thriller. Give it a try!

Cats in the Corner[2]

Number of kids: at least 4

Ages: any

Time allotted: 45 minutes or more

Space /Area: a wide open area where a square field can be defined

Equipment: one dodgeball for every four players

Description:

Startup: Players should define a large square field with four distinct corners. One out of every four people is chosen to be in the middle. Each of these players starts with a ball and must stand in the very center of the square. Everyone else is "cats" and they all go to the same corner to begin.

Object: As a cat: to be the last cat in the game.
Players in the middle: to hit the most cats.

Play: Once everyone is ready, one of the players in the middle announces loudly "cats get a corner". The cats must then all run to the next corner. They can run fast or slow, individually or in a big group, but they all must run in the same direction towards the same corner. While the cats are between corners, the people in the middle are trying to hit them with their dodgeballs. While the cats are still on a corner, they cannot be hit. The players in the middle must stay in the center of the square while throwing. If a cat is hit with a ball, that player is out and must go sit by the person who hit him or her. Once all the cats have safely arrived at the next corner or been hit and seated, a player in the middle again announces "cats get a corner". The cats run to the next corner and the process repeats itself. This continues until only one cat is left. The last cat is the winner of the cats. The person in the middle who knocked out the most cats is the winner in the middle. Choose new players for the middle and begin again. If there is only enough players for one person to be in the middle, the last cat is the winner and begins the next round in the middle.

Personal Comments: This game was a gym class favorite, but does not have to be played in gym. Any open yard of field can be used. Use strategy as a cat. Hide behind other cats and use skillful dodging. It is also fun to be in the middle trying to peg all your friends. The more people, the better, but this is still fun with just a few. This game can be played enjoyably for a long time, give it a shot!

Chicago

Number of kids: at least 2

Ages: 7 and up

Time allotted: 30 minutes or more

Space/Area: any area with a basketball hoop

Equipment: one basketball

Description:

Startup: Choose the area to play and decide which player gets the ball first. Make sure the area has a marked free throw line. Choosing the first player can be done with a shoot out at the free throw line.

Object: To be the first player to score twenty-one points.

Play: The player with the ball "checks" it and the game begins. Checking is done by passing the ball to another player and he or she passes it back. Each player is then trying to score twenty-one points. Using basic basketball rules, if any player makes a basket, he or she earns two or three points accordingly. Fouls also apply, as in regular basketball. The trick to this game is after a player makes a basket. That player then gets a chance to shoot free throws (each worth one point). If that player makes his or her first free throw, he or she keeps shooting, up to three times. If that player makes all three free throws, then that player checks the ball and the game continues. If that player misses a free throw, any player may get the rebound. The ball must then be dribbled back to the three point line and the game continues. This continues until one player has reached twenty-one points exactly. If a player goes over twenty-one, then that player's score returns to eleven and the game continues. The first player to reach exactly twenty-one points is the winner.

Personal Comments: Another basketball game of non-stop excitement! Great for basketball skills and fun, competitive exercise. Even if you are not that great at basketball, this game is great to try! Strategies and free throw shooting are the key. For example, if you have nineteen points, missing a free throw on purpose may not be a bad idea. If you have eighteen, just going for three pointers might be best, unless you really trust yourself at that free throw line. You do not want to get stuck at twenty! Get a bunch of people and try this game!

Club Ball

Number of kids: at least 4

Ages: any

Time allotted: 20 minutes or more

Space /Area: any open area

Equipment: one playground ball and one club, cone, or pin

Description:

Startup: Players should form a circular or square boundary and place the "club" in the middle. Players choose one person to be the first "protector". The protector enters the playing boundaries with the ball. Everyone else gathers outside the boundary.

Object: To knock over the club and be the protector.

Play: The protector starts the game by rolling the ball out of the playing area. Without entering the boundary, each player tries to obtain the ball. Then by ROLLING the ball, or kicking it softly, players try to knock the club over. The protector can do anything necessary within the boundaries to block the ball and keep it from knocking down the club. The protector cannot touch the club itself. If the ball is blocked or misses the club, another player grabs it and tries to knock over the club. Players are not allowed to enter the designated boundaries at any time. If the protector grabs the ball or if it stops inside the boundaries, the protector must toss it out to an outside player. If a player causes the club to fall, by hitting it with the ball or causing the protector to knock it over, then that player becomes the protector and a new round begins. If a player does this from inside the circle, it does not count; the club is set back up, and play resumes. Play several rounds.

Personal Comments: Make sure everyone gets a chance to be protector at least once. This actually gets pretty intense. Run around a lot and try to fake out the protector. The harder you play, the more fun it is!
If you like this, see also: Stride Club Bowl[3] and Standing Nutmeg

Dare Goal[3]

Number of kids: 2 teams of 3 or more

Ages: any

Time allotted: 40 minutes or more

Space /Area: a large, open grassy area or field

Equipment: none

Description:

Startup: Players should designate boundaries in a field that consists of two goal lines about 60 feet apart. Each goal line should have a "prison" behind it. Players choose teams and each team selects a captain. The teams split up and each team goes to opposite goal lines.

Object: To imprison all of the other team.

Play: Everyone lines up along their goal line and the captain of one team chooses a challenger from his own team. This player walks across the field to the other team's goal line. Everyone on this team then holds out their right hand with their right elbow touching their side. The challenging player then walks down the line of the opposing team touching their out held hands. The challenging player may touch the hands in any order and may touch only the hands that he or she chooses. Whenever this player wishes, he or she slaps one of the hands fairly hard. The player whose hand was slapped becomes the chaser and attempts to tag the challenger. Once the slap is made, the challenger must run back to his or her goal line without being tagged by the slapped player. If the challenger is successful, his or her team may choose to imprison the chaser or free an imprisoned member of their own team. If the challenger is tagged, the chaser's team gets to imprison the challenger. Being imprisoned means that player must stand in the other team's prison until freed or until the round ends. The other captain then selects a challenger and the same process occurs. This continues until one team has imprisoned all the members of the other team. The team who captures all the other players wins.

Personal Comments: This is a great running and chasing game. Players have the fun of challenging each other and faking people out with phony slaps. This games promotes high intensity action and can be fun for hours!!

Follow the Leader

Number of kids: at least 2

Ages: any

Time allotted: 20 minutes or more

Space /Area: a playground or a safe area with various obstacles

Equipment: none

Description:

Startup: Players chose an "It" to be the leader. Everyone forms a single file line behind the leader.

Object: To keep up with the leader, mimicking him or her as precisely as possible.

Play: There really are no stringent rules. Once everyone is in line, the leader should do difficult physical tasks, such as climbing over objects or weaving through them. Every other player must follow and mimic the leader as closely as possible.
    If competition is necessary, a player can be eliminated if he or she makes a mistake and does not follow the leader correctly. The last remaining child is the next leader.
    Otherwise, kids can just take turns leading for awhile. If players goof up, no big deal, they just keep following as closely as they can. Play ends when everyone wishes to stop.

Personal comments: The most simple, classic game around, but still a good one! It is best on playgrounds or an area with a lot of obstacles to trip up all the followers. This game is classically for younger kids, but older kids can do more challenging tasks to make it fun for them as well.

Four Corners (also called Army-Navy or Scramble)

Number of kids: at least 5

Ages: any

Time allotted: 20 minutes or more

Space /Area: a large square area where players can designate four corners or bases

Equipment: none

Description:

Startup: Players should designate a large square playing area with four corners or bases. One player is picked as the "caller" at the beginning of each game. The caller stands out of bounds for the entire round. Everyone else gets into the middle of the square.

Object: To be the last player in the game.

Play: Rules are picked for each of the four corners. Four standard rules are:
Corner 1: The last person to get to this corner and sit down is out.
Corner 2: Each player must get to the corner, hold hands with one partner and sit down. The person left with no partner is out or the last pair to sit down is out.
Corner 3: Same as corner 2, but players must form groups of 3.
Corner 4: Players must run to this corner, spin 10 times, and then sit down. The last person to do so is out.

The beautiful part about this game is those rules can be changed if desired. Kids can have fun making up crazy rules for each corner. The important thing is to make sure everyone knows which corners are 1, 2, 3, and 4, AND which rule applies to which corner. Once everything is determined, the players all get together in the middle and the caller yells out a number (1, 2, 3, or 4). Everyone but the caller must rush to that corner and follow the rule that applies. Whoever is eliminated moves out of bounds and waits for the next game. Everyone else moves back into the center and the caller yells out a corner and the process repeats itself. The last person left is the winner and becomes the caller for the next round.

Personal Comments: This game is awesome. Unfortunately, I never played this as a kid, but learned it recently with my tennis students. All the kids love it because each time you go to a corner it is madness! Mix up the rules a little, but try to stay somewhat consistent to avoid too much confusion. Round up all the kids you can and play this, they will love it!

Fox and Geese[1]

Number of kids: at least 2

Ages: any

Time allotted: 15 minutes or more

Space /Area: a large paved area that can be drawn on with chalk

Equipment: one piece of chalk

Description:

Startup: One player should draw a large circle with chalk that has 4 evenly spaced lines running through it, so it looks likes a sliced pizza. One players is chosen to be the "fox" The fox stands is the center of the chalked area. Everyone else, the "geese", spreads out on the circle.

Object: To avoid being the fox.

Play: The fox counts out loud to 3 and the game begins. A regular game of tag is then played, with some twists. All players, including the fox, must remain on the drawn lines. Players may go around the circle or through it on any drawn line. If a player is tagged or does not stay on the lines, that player becomes the fox. He or she then pauses, counts aloud to 3, and the game continues. Play continues until players wish to stop.

Option: With a smaller playing field, running should not be allowed. This will stop players from flying off the lines.

Personal comments: This is a great version of tag. It is challenging to stay on the lines when being chased. Also, watch out for people walking towards you on your line because it is very difficult to pass someone without stepping off the lines. Try it and see for yourself!

Freeze Tag

Number of kids: at least 3

Ages: any

Time allotted: 20 minutes or more

Space /Area: a decent sized grassy area

Equipment: none

Description:

Startup: Players should define boundaries and choose an "It".

Object: To avoid being It.

Play: Everyone spreads out in bounds. The It counts out loud to a certain number and the game begins. The It then attempts to tag everyone. If a player is tagged, that player must freeze where he or she was tagged. A player automatically becomes unfrozen as soon as any other player (except the It) touches him or her in any way. The round ends when one person has been tagged three times, or the It somehow freezes everyone. In the event that a player is tagged three times, that player is It the next round. If the It manages to freeze everyone (a rarity), the round ends and the current It chooses the next It.

Personal comments: A small area is good for this game, or else it is too hard for the It. Do not let people sit unfrozen, or they will never become it! Unfreeze them as soon as possible, so they can get tagged again! This is pretty high intensity and fun!

Variant: Tunnel Tag: This game is similar, except when a player gets tagged, that player must stand in place with his or her legs spread. Players are only unfrozen when another player crawl through their legs. If a player is tagged halfway through someone's legs, the player that was frozen is freed and the tagged player is then frozen in that spot. All other rules apply.

Hit or Run[3]

Number of kids: at least 7, or 6 and 1 adult

Ages: any

Time allotted: 30 minutes or more

Space /Area: any decent sized, open yard or field

Equipment: two dodgeballs

Description:

Startup: Players should designate two lines, separated by a decent sized field, and a box in the middle that extends across the field. Players should also place the two balls in the middle of this box and choose two teams. One person must be designated to call numbers. The caller then assigns a number, 1 through "x", to the players on each team ("x" being the number of players on each team). Each team proceeds to opposing ends of the field. The caller remains on the side of the field.

Object: To be on the first team to get 10 points.

Play: Once everyone is ready, the caller will yell out a number, 1 thru "x". There should be one person on each team with that number. These two run toward the middle box. The object then is for one player to grab a ball and return it to his or her sideline safely. There are two options in this game, however, once a player grabs a ball. Once a player leaves the center box with a ball, he or she is opened to be pegged by the other player. A player with a ball may either run back to his or her own goal line or he or she can try to peg the other player with the ball. A player cannot be pegged until he or she has left the center box with a ball. Any throw must come from within the center box. If a player is pegged, the pegger's team gets a point. If no one gets pegged, it is simply the first player who crosses his or her goal line with a ball earns a point. After a point is earned, the players return and the process repeats. The game is over once a team reaches a certain number of points (usually 10).

Personal comments: This game requires very high intensity and is exciting to play. Be risky, but safe at the same time. Try to grab your ball fast so you have the decision to break for it or begin a showdown. This is a little more oriented towards older kids, but anyone can play. The caller should try to give everyone have an equal turn trying to break for the middle.

Hot Box

Number of kids: at least 4

Ages: 6 and up

Time allotted: 30 minutes or more

Space /Area: a wide strip of grassy area, at least 20 feet long, or any large, open grassy area

Equipment: two "bases" (e.g. Frisbees), a ball to toss such as a tennis ball, or two gloves and a baseball or softball

Description:

Startup: The bases up are set up around twenty to thirty feet apart. Two people are chosen to be the throwers. Everyone else is a runner.

Object: For runners: to not get tagged.
For throwers: to tag or peg the runners.

Play: Each thrower stands in front of one base. The runners split up and get on one of the two bases. The throwers begin by tossing the ball back and forth. The runners then attempt to run back and forth between the bases anytime they feel they can do so without getting tagged. Whenever the runners are off base, the throwers try to tag them with the ball or peg them with it (**pegging is only allowed if a soft ball is chosen**). If a baseball or softball and gloves are used, only tagging with the glove is allowed. Each time a runner is tagged off of the bases, one point is added to that player's tally. If a runner is tagged off of base a certain number of times (usually 3), that runner becomes the thrower and the person who has been throwing the longest becomes a runner. For the first switch, whoever tagged the runner last is the one who switches. After each switch, every runner's tally (number of times tagged) resets to zero, and the game continues as before. The game ends whenever the players feel like quitting.

Personal comments: Another one of the greatest games in this book. A childhood favorite! Play this one!! While playing, be risky! The more risky the runners are, the more fun it is to run. If you are throwing, mix up the throws to lure people off base: throw high balls, grounders, or drop the ball on purpose. Everybody will like this game!

Infiltration[4]

Number of kids: 2 teams of 4 or more

Ages: any

Time allotted: at least 1 hour

Space /Area: a large field with some obstacles (best at night or dusk)

Equipment: two flashlights

Description:

Startup: Players should define rectangular boundaries around a field about 100 yards long and fairly wide. A middle line is then defined on the field. Two teams are formed and one player from each team is assigned to be a guard. The guards each get one flashlight. The guards remain on the middle line while each team goes to opposite ends of the field.

Object: To score 10 points first.

Play: When everyone is in position, the guards announce "Go!" and the game begins. Players then try to cross the middle line without getting spotted by the guard of the other team. Players can travel by any means (crawling, running, etc.). The guards try to shine their flashlights on the incoming opponents, but should not keep their flashlights on all the time. If the guards spot someone, the guard should announce it loudly and that person has to start over at their end of the field. If a player successfully passes the middle line without being spotted, that player should yell "Infiltration!" loudly and his or her team earns one point. That player must then go back to the end of the field to try to score again. Play does not stop when someone scores, but constantly continues. When one team earns 10 points, they win. Choose new guards, or mix up teams and play again!

Personal Comments: This is a fun game for older kids, but anyone can play. Try to be sneaky, but also make fast runs as well. It is harder to be the guard than you might think. The wider the field and the more obstacles on it, the easier it is to score, so adjust as necessary. Dress dark and really get into this game and it will be a blast!

Knockout

Number of kids: at least 4

Ages: any

Time allotted: 15 minutes or more

Space /Area: any area with a basketball hoop

Equipment: two basketballs

Description:

Startup: Players should choose an order and get in a single file line beginning at the foul line. The first two players each get one ball.

Object: To be the last player remaining.

Play: The first player in line shoots the ball. After the first player shoots, the second player may shoot. If any player misses the shot, he or she is allowed to move anywhere in order to rebound the ball and put it in the hoop. When a player makes his or her shot, that player must get the rebound and pass their ball to whoever is currently next in line. The first shot from every player must come from the foul line. The trick is that two players are always trying to make a basket at the same time. Whichever player is ahead in the order must make their ball first. If, at any point, a player makes a basket before the person in front of him or her, the player that got beat is knocked out of the game. The game is then paused, the balls are given to the next two players in line, and it all begins again. The last player left at the end is the winner.

Personal comments: Takes some basketball skill, but also a lot of speed and intensity. Fun, high paced action. Give it a try!

Last Man Tag[3]

Number of kids: 2 teams of 3 or more

Ages: any

Time allotted: at least 45 minutes

Space /Area: a large, open grassy area

Equipment: none

Description:

Startup: Players should define boundaries that consist of two large bases, located about 50 feet apart. Teams are chosen and go to opposing bases.

Object: To eliminate all the players on the other team.

Play: Everyone attempts to tag people on the other team. A player can only be tagged if he or she is off their base. Players may leave their base at any time. The trick is (read carefully), to be able to tag an opponent, the tagger must have left base AFTER the opponent left his or her base (this sounds complicated, but is simple when put into play). Safety can be attained by returning to base or by successfully making a tag. Any tagged player is eliminated from the game. A successful tagger is temporarily safe, but must return to his or her base immediately (to indicate a safe return, a player should hold both hands in the air while transitioning back to base). Upon reaching base, the tagger can then attempt another tag, but is again unsafe upon leaving base. Play does not stop when a tag is made. Play is continuous and tagging can occur anytime a player is not safe. Play continues until one team has had all their players eliminated.

Personal Comments: Players should both lure out their opponents and aggressively try to tag. You would not believe how much fun this can be! Do NOT hide on base all day. The more time you spend in the playing area trying to lure others off base or trying to tag someone, the more fun it is. Be aggressive and risky and have fun! Go try this game!

Link Tag

Number of kids: at least 6

Ages: any

Time allotted: at least 20 minutes

Space /Area: any decent sized open area

Equipment: none

Description:

Startup: Players should define boundaries, choose a "chaser", and choose a "runner". Everyone else then finds a partner. The pairs should spread out in bounds and stand with their elbows linked together.

Object: To avoid being It.

Play: Everyone spreads out in bounds. The chaser counts out loud to a certain number and the game begins. The chaser is always in pursuit of the runner. If the runner is tagged, he or she then becomes the chaser and the chaser becomes the runner. At any time, the runner may link elbows with someone. If the runner links with a pair, the person on the other side of that linked duo must break off and become the runner. A runner may be chased as long as he or she desires before linking. Tag backs are allowed, meaning that if the chaser tags the runner, the two immediately trade places and the game continues. The game ends when everyone decides to quit.

Options: If someone is watching or wants to sit out, that person can be given the power to call "switch" at any time. When "switch" is called, whoever is the runner immediately becomes the chaser and vice versa. This is especially advisable with an odd number of kids. With an odd number, twos runner may also be opted.

Personal comments: This game is fun for a little chaos, but is very safe and enjoyable. Switching is hilarious to watch if used, but this game is always a wild time!

No Touch Ground

Number of kids: 1 or more

Ages: any

Time allotted: 20 minutes or more

Space /Area: a playground or a safe area with many obstacles

Equipment: none

Description:

Startup: Players should find a good area to play. One player then chooses a starting point and a destination.

Object: To reach the chosen destination without touching the ground.

Play: There are not too many rules in this game, except trying not to touch the ground. An exact path does not have to be followed, but can be. The chooser usually starts off, and the others may follow or make their own path. Usually one path will be simplest to one destination. When everyone reaches the destination, have a new player choose another destination and proceed as before.

If competition is necessary, a rule can be applied where any player that does touch the ground is eliminated. Whoever gets closest to the destination without touching ground is the winner, and chooses the next destination. If multiple players complete the course, they are all winners.

Personal comments: This game requires a good combination of dexterity and strength. It is fun because it always changes and is never the same. Simple, but has endless possibilities, and has always been a popular choice for kids. The more challenging the course, the more fun it will be!

Variant: A leader can also be chosen, such as in Follow the Leader. Those rules apply and if one touches the ground while following the leader, that player is eliminated.

Red Light, Green Light

Number of kids: 3 or more

Ages: any

Time allotted: 20 minutes or more

Space /Area: a straight path on any surface

Equipment: none

Description:

Startup: Players should choose a playing area and a starting line, then pick an "It". The It walks back from the starting line as far as he of she sees fit. Everyone else lines up on the starting line waiting for the game to begin.

Object: To be the first player to reach the It.

Play: The game begins when the It calls "Green Light". Everyone is allowed to advance off the line towards the It as fast as possible. When the It calls "Red Light", everyone must stop immediately. Those who do not stop right away are forced to move back as far as the It deems necessary. The It then calls "Green Light" again and everyone else again begins to run until the It calls "Red Light". This repeats until one player reaches and tags the It. This player is the winner and becomes It for the next round.

Personal comments: It is fun to be a ruthless It, penalizing and teasing the player's with fast stop's and go's. It is also fun to be a runner, and stop and go and fall over trying to stop. Play several rounds. This game is most fun once the players get the hang of being It.

Relays

Number of kids: at least 2 teams of 2 or more

Ages: usually any, depends on relay

Time allotted: 20 minutes or more

Space /Area: depends on relay chosen

Equipment: depends on relay chosen

Description:

Startup: Players should choose a type of relay and teams are chosen accordingly.

Object: To win the relay by finishing first or the fastest.

Play: A list of all possible relays would be far too extensive because any simple task may be turned into a relay. An example is placing four balls in a large square pattern. The first person must pick up all four balls, one at a time, and hand them to the next person in line. That second person then must put them back one at a time, returning to the starting point after setting down each ball. After each player has gone once, the team who finishes first wins.

Bike races around blocks, dribbling tennis balls up and down a driveway, climbing around a jungle gym, and throwing a Frisbee down three yards and back were all fun ideas we used to do. Also, any sort of funny body position or teamwork task can be used. Teams can race all at once or can take turns and time each other. Whoever finishes the relay first or fastest is the winner. The winning team can pick the next type of relay.

Personal comments: Be creative. This idea presents literally thousands of games alone and may be used every day. Parents can help or kids can make up their own. We used to do relays for hours, just making them up and doing them on the spot. Start trying this. Everyone will get into the idea of creating and performing relays and fun creativity will follow. Relays can promote team effort, fun competition, and good exercise.

Rim Game

Number of kids: 2 or more

Ages: 7 or older

Time allotted: 40 minutes or more

Space /Area: a driveway or cement area with a basketball hoop

Equipment: one basketball

Description:

Startup: If there is no foul box, a box must be drawn by chalk on the ground of about the same size. If a driveway has squares in its design, that can also work well. That is the boundaries. Choose an order of players.

Object: To give others points, while surviving and keeping one's own points to a minimum.

Play: The first player starts on the foul line (or end of the box) and tosses the basketball so that it hits the rim of the basketball hoop. The next player must then gain possession of the ball. This player may then move around freely within the designated box. The player with the ball does not have to dribble, and the other players do not guard him or her. While staying anywhere in bounds, he or she then throws the ball against any part of the rim, by any means desired. The next player then catches the ball and repeats the process, and so on.

     The trick and skill to the game comes within the narrower rules and point scoring. After the ball is thrown by a player, it must strike some part of the RIM (backboard alone does not count) and the ball must land within bounds. If the ball misses the rim and lands out of bounds or lands out of bounds after hitting the rim, the player that threw the ball out of bounds (off the rim or not) loses the point. When a player loses a point, one point is added to that player's tally (a tally is the number of points lost).

     If the ball DOES land in bounds after hitting the rim, it is then the next person's turn. The next player in order must then catch the ball before it goes out of bounds. He or she can catch the ball before or after it bounces, but must NOT step out of bounds, like regular basketball. A jumping save may be made (as in regular basketball), as long as the ball never lands out of bounds and as long as the player never touches the ball while he or she is out of bounds. If a save is made, the player still must obtain possession of the ball before it goes back out of the box. If a fair ball does go out of bounds or an illegal save is made when it becomes someone's turn (as described), that player loses the point. It remains a player's turn until that player successfully catches and throws the ball against the rim of the basket. It then becomes the next person's turn, and so on. Whenever a point is lost, play stops, and the next player in order begins a new point at the foul line as before. A player is eliminated when he or she loses 5 or 10 points (determined at the start). Play continues until only one player is left.

A redo can be declared if the ball or one's running path is interfered with by another player, etc. Interference with another player or his or her ball in NEVER allowed. Players must do their best to avoid the ball when it is not their turn. An optional rule may even be played that states: the point is lost by a player if the ball strikes that player when it is not his or her turn.

Personal comments: Perhaps the BEST game in this book! A must try! This is one my brother Chris and I created one summer day. It is an absolute blast, especially once you get the hang of it. It will seems a little complicated from simply reading the rules alone, but try playing it….it will not be as difficult as it seems. My personal favorite! The more you play, the more strategy you learn, and the more fun it can be. It is entertainment for years!!!

Roof Game

Number of kids: 2 or more (with 4 or more, divide into teams)

Ages: any

Time allotted: 15 minutes or more

Space /Area: a slanted roof with no gutter that has room to run in front of it (a roof with a gutter can be used with a large, soft ball that will not get caught in or damage the gutter)

Equipment: a semi-bouncy ball, such as a tennis ball

Description:

Startup: The trick is finding a good roof that works. Players then choose an order if there are more than two players or teams. Players should also define boundaries on the roof if it is well over twenty feet long.

Object: To give others points, while surviving and keeping one's own points to a minimum.

Play: The person who is first in order gets the ball and tosses it onto the roof from anywhere in any manner chosen (high and bouncy, low and hard, etc.). The ball must land on the roof and also return off the front of the roof (not off one of the sides or out of the designated area). An illegal throw causes the thrower to lose the point. Every time a legal throw is made, the next player must then catch the ball before it hits the ground. If the ball is caught, that player throws it onto the roof for the next player to catch. If the ball is dropped, the player who was supposed to catch it loses the point. When a player loses a point, one point is added to that player's tally (a tally is the number of points lost). A player is eliminated upon reaching 5 points. A new game may then be started or play may continue until only one player is left.

Personal comments: Opposite to what you might think, the trick to this game is not in the catching, but in the throwing. Try throwing the ball with spins or bounces that make it difficult to catch, or perhaps throwing it so it barely touches the top of the roof then falls down. This is a very simple game for all ages, but do not let its simplicity fool you. It is surprisingly challenging and exciting!

Spinning Rope

Number of kids: at least 3

Ages: any

Time allotted: 15 minutes or more

Space /Area: a decent sized paved or hard and smooth surface

Equipment: one long jump rope (or a rope with a small weight on one end)

Description:

Startup: Players choose an "It" and he or she starts in the middle of the others, holding one end of the rope. The other players line up around the It, staying within the length of the rope.

Object: Not to get hit by the rope.

Play: The It grabs one end of the rope and begins spinning so that the rope also spins along the ground (not in the air) in a big circle. The others players must jump the rope without it touching them. The It may slow down, speed up, move the rope up and down (a little), etc. to try to mess up the jumpers. When a person is hit by the rope, that player becomes the new It and play continues. The game ends whenever the players agree to stop.

Personal Comments: Simple, but a good time. Good for kids of mixed ages.

Sprite Ball[3]

Number of kids: at least 5

Ages: any

Time allotted: 40 minutes or more

Space /Area: any large, open area

Equipment: one dodgeball

Description:

Startup: Players should choose an "It" and define a square field with two distinct end lines and a center area for the It to stand in. The It stands in the middle area and everyone else splits evenly behind the two end lines of the field.

Object: To avoid becoming It.

Play: Once everyone is ready, the It announces a player's name. That player then calls out the name of a player on the opposing end line. These players must instantly step across the end line into bounds. They must then trade places by crossing to the other side of the field. Without leaving the center circle, the It tries to hit either of the two players with the ball as they cross the field. Players may run anywhere in bounds to try to dodge the ball. If a player is hit with the ball, he or she becomes It for the next round. If both players cross successfully, the It remains in place and another round begins.

Personal Comments: This is a great variant of Cats in the Corner[1]. Use strategy in who's name to call and when running. It is fun to run and dodge, but also to be in the middle trying to peg all your friends. The more people, the better, but this is still fun with just a few. This game can be played enjoyably for a long time, give it a shot!

Statues

Number of kids: 3 or more

Ages: any

Time allotted: 20 minutes or more

Space /Area: a decent sized, grassy, open area

Equipment: none

Description:

Startup: Players should define boundaries choose a Judge.

Object: To be the last player in the game.

Play: Everyone but the Judge begins to move about randomly within the defined area. The Judge yells "Freeze!" at will, whereupon everyone must freeze instantly…like statues. Failing to freeze instantly results in elimination from the game. The players must hold their position until approved by the Judge. The Judge walks around and asks what each "statue" is posing as. If an acceptable answer is given by all and no one falls, "Unfreeze!" is called by the Judge and everyone begins moving again. If anyone falls, cannot hold their statue position, or the Judge does not think their answer justifies their pose, that player is eliminated. The Judge is responsible for ALL elimination decisions. The last person remaining wins and is Judge for the next round.

Personal Comments: This game forces you to be creative. Move around as randomly as possible so you can get yourself into crazy positions. Be creative with your responses and if you are the Judge, knock people out who are not creative because you have the final say!

Variant: Red Light, Green Light Statues: This variant simply adds an important rule to Red Light, Green Light. When "Red Light" is called, everyone must stop immediately and hold their position, as statues. Similar to "Statues", if a player moves before "Green Light" is called, then that player must start over at the beginning (but is not eliminated). Each person must also call out what they are posing as in their statue position. The It, or Judge, may make a player start over for a bad answer as well. Then "Green Light" is called again and play continues. All other rules of Red Light, Green Light apply.

Steal the Bacon

Number of kids: at least 7, or 6 and 1 adult

Ages: any

Time allotted: 30 minutes or more

Space /Area: a decent sized, open yard or field

Equipment: an item to be grabbed, such as a handkerchief or piece of rope

Description:

Startup: Players should designate two lines, separated by a decent sized field, and place the "bacon" in the middle. Players should also choose two teams and designate one separate person to call numbers. The caller then assigns a number, 1 through "x", to the players on each team ("x" being the number of players on each team). Each team proceeds to opposing ends of the field. The caller remains on the side of the field.

Object: To be on the first team to get 10 points.

Play: Once everyone is ready, the caller yells out a number, 1 thru "x". There should be one person on each team with that number. These two run toward the "bacon". The object is for one player to grab the bacon and return it to his or her sideline without being tagged by the other player. Either player may grab the bacon, but does not have to grab it. A player cannot be tagged until the bacon is grabbed. If a player grabs the bacon and makes it back to his or her line without being tagged, that team earns a point. If the player is tagged before making it back, the tagger's team scores the point. Once the bacon is grabbed, it cannot be dropped. After a point is earned by a team, the bacon is placed back in the middle, the players return to their side, and the caller calls another number. Once a certain number of points is reached by a team (usually 10), that team is the winner.

Personal comments: This is very exciting to play. Be risky. You can try to grab the bacon fast or you can circle like a showdown. Good for all ages. The caller should try to give everyone have an equal chance to steal. High intensity and fun!

Stride Club Bowl[3]

Number of kids: at least 4

Ages: any

Time allotted: 20 minutes or more

Space /Area: any open area

Equipment: one identical club, cone, or pin for each child and one or more playground balls (depending on the number of players) (or see Standing Nutmeg below for play without clubs)

Description:

Startup: Everyone stands in a circle with their feet spread wide. The circle should be formed with everyone's feet touching toe to toe with the person next to them. Each player places his or her club directly between his or her feet.

Object: To be the last remaining player.

Play: The ball(s) is given to a player at random. One player says "Ready, Set, Go!" and the game begins. Pushing and shoving are not allowed. Moving one's foot and throwing the ball are also not allowed. Otherwise, players should do whatever they can to knock over their opponents' club with a ball. Players should also be sure to protect their own club. The ball must be rolled or pushed through the hands of a player to knock down the club. If a player's club is knocked over or a player moves his or her feet without getting pushed, that player is eliminated. Only ONE player may be eliminated at a time. If two pins are knocked down at similar times, only the player whose pin was knocked over first is out. As soon as one player is eliminated, the game is paused and a smaller circle is formed in the same fashion. The player who caused the elimination begins with the ball and says "Ready, Set, Go!". The whole process repeats. This continues until only one player is left. That player is the winner and begins with the ball the next round.

Personal Comments: You don't run much in this game, but it will wear you out faster than you think. It is very high intensity, stressful, and fun at the same time! This is a different type of game then most people have played and is a riot to try.
If you like this, see also: Club Ball[1] and try the variants!

Variant: Standing Nutmeg: If no cones are available, or just for fun, try this version. The rules are the same, except players must roll or shove the ball all the way through another player's legs to eliminate them, instead of knocking over the opponent's club.

Variant: Brooklyn Bridge[1]: This game is similar to Standing Nutmeg, except players form two teams. These teams get into a side by side line, facing each other, and play team Standing Nutmeg. As players are eliminated, their team's line slides together to close the gap. The team with the last player(s) is the winner.

Tiger and Leopard[1]

Number of kids: at least 2

Ages: any

Time allotted: 15 minutes or more

Space /Area: any open field

Equipment: none

Description:

Startup: Players should choose a starting line and a finish line, then split themselves into "tigers" and "leopards". There should be a few more tigers than leopards.

Object: To be a leopard.

Play: Tigers line up on the starting line, facing the finish line. Leopards stand behind the tigers and chant "A tiger, a leopard, a tiger, a leopard, one of them crouches, the other leaps over". Upon hearing "one of them crouches", the tigers crouch all the way down and after finishing the chant, the leopards leap over any chosen tiger. The tigers that were leaped must then chase and tag the leopard who jumped over them. If the leopard crosses the finish line without being tagged, then that player remains a leopard. If a leopard is tagged, the tiger who tagged him or her becomes a leopard and the tagged leopard becomes a tiger. Players can play as many rounds as they desire.

Personal comments: A great game of tag, chase, and leap frog combined into one. Tons of exercise and a lot of fun.

Two-Man Basketball[3]

Number of kids: 2 teams of at least 3

Ages: any

Time allotted: 30 minutes or more

Space /Area: one half of a basketball court

Equipment: one basketball

Description:

Startup: Players should choose two teams and designate one person to call numbers. The caller then assigns a number, 1 through "x", to the players on each team ("x" being the number of players on each team). The teams then proceed to opposing sides of the basketball court.

Object: To be on the first team to get 10 points.

Play: When everyone is ready, the caller yells out one or two numbers (caller's choice) in the range 1 thru "x". There should be a person on each team with that number(s). As the caller yells the numbers, he or she bounces the basketball off the backboard hard and the point begins. The players that were called run to get possession of the ball and score. The first player or team to score gets the point for his or her team. Normal basketball rules apply (no pushing, no hacking, no double dribbling, no traveling, etc.) except that everyone is trying to score on the same basket. After a score is made, the players return to their sidelines, the caller calls another number(s) and the process repeats. This continues until one team scores 10 points and wins. After each game, a new person should be made caller.

If there is an even number of players, the ball can be set in the middle of the foul line and one player from each team should take turns calling the numbers.

Personal comments: This is exciting to play and works on basketball skills. Try to let everyone have an equal turn trying to score. This game is high intensity and fun!

Wall Ball

Number of kids: 2 or more

Ages: 6 and up

Time allotted: 25 minutes or more

Space/Area: any large wall with a paved area in front

Equipment: a semi-bouncy ball such as a tennis ball

Description:

Startup: Players should find a good, open wall and set boundaries on the pavement. Boundaries should be a good-sized area about 10 feet wide and 15 feet long. If there are more than two players, they must choose an order.

Object: To give others points, while surviving and keeping one's own points to a minimum.

Play: The first person begins by tossing the ball against the wall from anywhere he or she chooses. The trick is that after hitting the wall, the ball must land on the pavement within the designated boundaries. The next person must then catch the ball after one bounce or in the air. That player then throws the ball against the wall and the next person must catch it. If, at any time, the ball bounces twice on a fair throw, the player who is attempting to catch the ball loses the point. If one loses a point, that player adds one point to his or her tally (a player's tally is the number of points lost). If a throw bounces off the wall and LANDS out of bounds, the thrower gets the point. When 5 or 10 points is reached by one player, that player is out of the game. The last person left is the winner.

Personal Comments: This was actually a childhood and teenage favorite. It sounds simple, but can be a lot more fun and complex than you might imagine. This is a good, simple, and relatively unstructured game that is good for just goofing around with friends. If played seriously, it can also be high intensity with lots of funny incidents and skilled points. Definitely worth a try!

Activity Level III

1, 2, 3…I spy

Number of kids: at least 4

Ages: any

Time allotted: at least 45 minutes

Space /Area: several connecting neighborhood yards (front and back) or a large area with places to hide

Equipment: none

Description:

Startup: Players should define boundaries, choose a base (such as a porch or fence), and select an "It".

Object: To avoid being It.

Play: The It guarding the base closes his or her eyes and counts to a number, usually 50, to give the other players a chance to disperse and hide. The It then tries to do two things: find the other players and protect the base. The other players also have two goals: not to be spotted and to reach base before "being called".

Being called: If the It sees someone at any time, to "call" that player the It MUST return to base and while maintaining contact with it, yell loudly "one, two, three, I spy _____" (and yells the player's name and location, example: Jane behind the red car). If the It is correct in naming the player and their location, the game is over. That named player is It the next round and the game restarts. If the It is wrong, play resumes (guessing is not allowed!!).

During the time that the It is trying to find people, the other players are waiting for a chance to break towards base. If a player can touch the base and yells "safe" before being called, that player is safe and watches until the next round. The It may "call" a player running towards base by saying "one, two, three, I spy _____ running in". The It must complete the whole phrase loudly before that person contacts the base and yells "safe".

Again, the round ends as soon as one person is successfully called. That person is It for the next round. Everyone still hiding is called to return to base and the new round begins. If everyone reaches base safely, the It is It once more unless someone volunteers to take the It's place.

Personal comments: A childhood top 5! Everyone loved it! This game can be played at day or night for hours. Try it!!! It requires some honesty about where one is spotted, but watch for technicalities. Be honest and admit if you are accurately "called", but if you are It, do not get upset if you are wrong. Trust that the other player is not lying. For example, you may call a player as being in the side yard, but by the time you call it, they may in the back yard, etc.

If you are It, be aggressive. Do not just sit on base waiting for players, but be careful not to wander too far. Guard the base, but search for people as well. If you a runner, be aggressive. Breaking for the base is the biggest thrill in the game! Try this game and you will be hooked!

Army[1]

Number of kids: at least 2

Ages: any

Time allotted: 15 minutes or more

Space /Area: any large area with obstacles and places to hide

Equipment: players' choice - anything that could be used in a pretend battle (plastic guns, water guns, cap guns, even sticks that can be pretend guns)

Description:

Startup: Players should define boundaries, gather any desired equipment, and split up into two teams.

Object: To win the fake battle.

Play: There are not too many rules to this game. Players simply spread out within boundaries and the battle begins. Players should try to sneak up on each other and yell "Bang" with their weapon pointed at an opponent. If an opponent is "hit", he or she lies down and plays dead until the battle has ended. The winner is the team who has the last remaining players.

Personal comments: This game is fun if children really get into it. Pretend you are really in battle mode, use your imagination, and go play.

Ball Punch[1]

Number of kids: at least 5

Ages: any

Time allotted: 15 minutes or more

Space /Area: any small open area

Equipment: one large ball (such as a playground ball)

Description:

Startup: One player is chosen to be "It" and everyone else stands in a circle. The It begins outside the circle of players.

Object: To avoid being It.

Play: One player begins with the ball and must pass it to the player on his or her left. Players must then continue to pass the ball to the left. While this is occurring, the It is trying to punch the ball while it is being passed. The It cannot hit the ball out of anyone's hands, but can hit it anytime it is in the air or on the ground. The It must also remain outside the circle at all times. If the It successfully interrupts a pass by hitting the ball, the player who allowed the hit to occur becomes It and must change places with the former It.

Personal comments: The size of the circle makes a large difference. Try changing the distance between players to find the best game. Overall, this is a fun, high paced game that's definitely worth a try.

Break and Run[4] (also called: Keeper and Bull)

Number of kids: at least 7

Ages: 8 and up

Time allotted: 30 minutes or more

Space /Area: any large open area

Equipment: none

Description:

Startup: Players pick one person to be the "bull" and another to be the "keeper". Everyone else forms a ring of people by joining hands or wrists. The bull gets into the middle of the ring, with the keeper on the outside.

Object: Bull and keeper's goal: to get the bull out of the ring.
Everyone else's goal: to keep the bull inside the ring, then tag the bull and keeper when the bull escapes.

Play: The keeper counts to three, says "go", and the game begins. The bull and the keeper then do whatever they can (without using violent measures) to get the bull out of the ring. Pushing, pulling, and dodging are all allowed, but being too physical is not. The bull and the keeper cannot team up against one player on the ring. The keeper also may never enter the ring. Players forming the ring may move or block the bull by any means necessary (without using violent measures, of course), but players cannot break the ring. Once the bull breaks loose, the bull and the keeper should run off as fast as possible. All the other players in the ring break apart and try to tag the keeper and bull. Whoever tags them takes their place in the next round. Since everyone will want to be bull, if a player has already been bull once, he or she should choose another player who has not.

Personal Comments: Red rover, tag, and wrestling all combined into one game!! This game is tough to beat if you have a decent amount of kids. This can provide hours of fun and almost never gets old. Do not be afraid to be physical in this game; if you are scared to be pushed a little, do not play. Try to round up a bunch of kids and try this one out!

Circle Chase[3]

Number of kids: at least 8

Ages: any

Time allotted: 25 minutes or more

Space /Area: any decent sized open area

Equipment: none

Description:

Startup: Players choose a "chaser" and a "runner". Everyone else gets into a circle, with the runner on the inside and the chaser on the outside.

Object: For the chaser to catch the runner

Play: Everyone in the circle joins hands. The runner says "Go" and the game begins. The chaser then tries to break into the circle to catch the runner. The circle should try to keep the chaser out (without getting rough). The runner may leave the circle to escape, but if he or she does, everyone in the circle drops hands. Upon the runner's reentrance, the circle players rejoin hands. This goes on until the chaser catches the runner. The runner and chaser then choose their replacements and another round ensues. Players can play as many rounds as desired.

Personal Comments: Fun to be part of the circle and to trap people in and out. Also fun to force your way in and out of the circle. Gets a little crazy, but a lot of fun!

Cowboys and Indians

Number of kids: 2 teams of at least 2

Ages: any

Time allotted: 20 minutes or more

Space /Area: any decent sized open area

Equipment: none

Description:

Startup: Players should define a field of play with two end lines and choose two even teams of "Cowboys" and "Indians". The Cowboys all line up on end line of the field and close their eyes. The Indians begin at the opposite end line on the field.

Object: The Cowboys are trying to capture all the Indians.

Play: Play begins when the Cowboys turn around and close their eyes and the Indians begin to move toward the Cowboys. The Indians are trying to get as close to the Cowboys as possible without being heard. The Cowboys, keeping their eyes closed, are trying to hear the Indians getting closer. At any time, a Cowboy may call out "Indians!". When "Indians!" is called, every Cowboy can open their eyes. The Cowboys then try to tag the Indians. The Indians must then run back to their end line on the field before being tagged. If an Indian is tagged, he or she is out of the game. If, however, an Indian should make it all the way across the field to the Cowboys' end line before "Indians!" is called, he or she cannot be tagged that round. The rounds continue until one Indian is left. That Indian is the winner. The Cowboys and Indians then switch teams and a new game is played.

Personal Comments: The trick to this game is being bold as an Indian and knowing when to call "Indians!" as a Cowboy. The bolder you are as an Indian, the more fun the game is. It is good to be daring and try to make it all the way across the field. Even if you do not, it is fun to get chased by all the Cowboys. If you are a Cowboy, the trick is not calling "Indians!" too early. Give the Indians a chance to act brave and to get close, then suddenly call "Indians!" and rush after them. Listen carefully to try to hear them getting near you. Let loose with this game and enjoy it!

Ghost in the Graveyard

Number of kids: at least 3

Ages: any

Time allotted: at least 45 minutes

Space /Area: several connecting neighborhood yards (front and back) or a large area with places to hide

Equipment: none

Description:

Startup: Players should define boundaries, "the graveyard", choose a base, such as a fence or lamppost, and select a "ghost".

Object: The ghost is trying to catch players before they reach base.

Play: The game begins when everyone but the ghost closes their eyes to count while the ghost runs and hides. The counting may be to 50, but traditionally is said aloud as follows:
"one o'clock, two o'clock, three o'clock o'rock…
four o'clock, five o'clock, six o'clock o'rock…
seven o'clock, eight o'clock, nine o'clock, o'rock…
ten o'clock, eleven o'clock, twelve o'clock, o'rock…….MIDNIGHT! (yelled)".
Then the players spread out, searching for the "ghost in the graveyard". If a player spots the ghost or if the ghost jumps out, the player who sees him or her first should instantly yell "Ghost in the graveyard!". Once this is called, everyone tries to reach base before being tagged by the ghost. If a player touches the base, they are safe from being tagged. The first player the ghost tags is the ghost for the next round. If everyone makes it to base safely, the same ghost hides again. Play continues until players choose to quit.

Personal comments: Another childhood top five!! Extremely fun at night, or at least when it is getting dark. This makes it easier to hide and a little more frightening and heart pounding. A really fun game if taken seriously. It is best where there are good places to hide, so it takes awhile to find the ghost. Also, be careful when searching, make sure the ghost cannot pop and get you!

Kick the Can

Number of kids: 2 teams of at least 2

Ages: any

Time allotted: at least 45 minutes

Space /Area: several connecting neighborhood yards (front and back) or a large area with places to hide

Equipment: one can

Description:

Startup: Players should set boundaries, choose two teams, and set the can in a safe place in the center of the boundaries. One team should be designated as the Kickers (offense) and one as the Chasers (defense).

Object: The Chasers are trying to tag all the Kickers, while the Kickers are trying to kick the can.

Play: The Chasers huddle around the can and close their eyes and counts to a number (usually 50) to give the Kickers a chance to disperse and hide. The Chasers then try to do two things: find and tag the Kickers, and protect the can. If a Chaser manages to tag a Kicker, that Kicker is out for the round and must wait on the side until the round ends. The Chasers win if all the Kickers are successfully caught before the can is kicked. If a Kicker manages to reach the can and kick it without being tagged, the game is over. The Kickers win. After a winner is found, everyone is called to return to the middle. Switch teams and begin a new round. One round at a time can be played, or the teams can play a series, in which a point is earned for every time the can is successfully kicked.

Personal comments: A, or perhaps, THE classic game! An extremely fun game for being as simple as it is! If you have never played this, get out there and try it. There is a reason it is such a classic: it is easy to play and is hours of fun!!

Manhunt

Number of kids: at least 5

Ages: 8 and up

Time allotted: an hour or more

Space /Area: at least an entire block or large forest area, etc. with hiding places and space to roam

Equipment: none

Description:

Startup: Players should define LARGE boundaries, usually a neighborhood block. Players should then choose a base and pick teams. One team is chosen to be the "Hunters" and the others are the "Prisoners". Usually 1 to 3 more players are chosen to be Hunters.

Object: For the Hunters to find and bring to base all the Prisoners.

Play: The Hunters remain on base for 3 minutes while the Prisoners run and hide anywhere within the boundaries chosen. The Hunters then split up and begin to look for the Prisoners. Prisoner's may stay on the move or hide, and if spotted, a Prisoner may run. To capture a Prisoner, the Hunter must wrap both arms around the Prisoner. The Prisoner must then accept capture and go with the Hunter back to base. The base then becomes the prison for the captured Prisoner. Jailbreaks are possible in this game, but only ONE Prisoner may be freed at a time. To free a Prisoner, another Prisoner must touch hands with a captured Prisoner. They both must then run off and may be captured at any time during this process. Since Prisoners are difficult to catch, these Prisoners cannot return right away to attempt to free more Prisoners, but must wait at least a few minutes. The game ends when all Prisoners have been successful caught on the Manhunt, or when the Hunters give up.

Personal comments: As Prisoners are captured, the right balance of Hunters must be found to guard the prison and to hunt. This is why it is usually better for more people to be on the Hunters' team. The BIGGER the boundaries, the BETTER. This game is supposed to be hard and take a long time. The idea is patience, good hiding, and pretending you are really hunting or being hunted. Take it seriously, hide well, and go have fun!!

Variants: Flashlights may be used to capture at night in place of wrapping arms around the Prisoner. Simply tagging Prisoners may also be used for capture, especially for younger children.

Variant: **Ringalevio**[1]: This is a similar game, but played in a smaller area (maybe two yards, front and back). The jail should be a larger circle in the middle of the playing field. To capture a Prisoner, they only need to be tagged. To free a Prisoner, an uncaptured Prisoner must enter the jail circle and yell the players name and Ringalevio. The game ends when all the Prisoner's are caught.

Maypole

Number of kids: at least 3

Ages: any

Time allotted: 20 minutes or more

Space /Area: a pole or an open tree trunk

Equipment: long strips of ribbon of equal length for each player

Description:

Startup: Each player gets a piece of ribbon and ties one end of it to the top of the pole. Players should then walk away from the pole, holding the other end of the ribbon so it stretches to full length. Players should spread out evenly around the pole.

Object: To decorate the pole.

Play: One player yells "Go!" and the game begins. Half of the players should begin running clockwise and the other half should run counter-clockwise around the pole. These players should weave inside and outside of each other in a random fashion. This will leave a great pattern of woven ribbons on the pole that all players can enjoy. The ribbon should be taken down when players are finished and multiple rounds can be played. Each round will leave a unique pattern!

Personal comments: A classic game that most children have never played. It is fairly simple and there is no competition. All players will enjoy this positive experience. If you have never done this, it is a must try!

One Man Toss Up[3]

Number of kids: at least 4

Ages: any

Time allotted: at least 30 minutes

Space /Area: a large open yard or field

Equipment: one soft ball

Description:

Startup: Players should choose a ball, define roughly circular boundaries, and pick one player to be the first "tosser".

Object: To avoid being the tosser.

Play: Everyone gathers near the tosser as he or she throws the ball into the air. The tosser then calls out a name and everyone scatters. The tosser then tries to run into a safe area away from other players, but must stay in bounds. The person whose name was called must get the ball and yell "STOP!". At this, everyone but the tosser must stop moving. The ball is then allowed to be passed three times, but may never touch the ground. The object is to try to hit the tosser (who is allowed to run and dodge) using three or less passes and a throw. If someone hits the tosser (before the ball hits the ground) then the tosser is it again. If not, the person who threw and missed the tosser or let the ball hit the ground is then the tosser for the next round. Play ends when all players agree to stop.

Personal Comments: Spread out!! Try to make it impossible for the tosser to escape. This is a great running and dodging game. Uses teamwork and individual effort. Loads of intensity, give it a try!!

Pass and Overtake[3]

Number of kids: at least 6

Ages: any

Time allotted: 20 minutes or more

Space /Area: any open area

Equipment: one ball

Description:

Startup: Everyone chooses an order and gets into a single file line, spaced about 4 feet apart. The first person in line takes the ball, chooses a spot about 15 feet straight in front of the line, and goes there to stand.

Object: For the chaser to catch the runner.

Play: The first person (who moved 15 feet up) begins by throwing the ball to the second player in line. These players then have a goal. The person who caught the ball becomes the runner. The runner must then run to the end of the line, weaving in and out of the people in line. The passer must try to catch the runner before he or she completes the trip. Neither player can move until the ball is passed and caught. If the passer catches the runner, he or she earns a point. If the runner escapes, the runner gets the point. After either result, the passer goes to the back of the line and the runner becomes the new passer. A round ends when every player has played both positions once. Play as many rounds as desired. The winner is the player with the most points at the end.

Personal Comments: Good for some fun bobbing and weaving. Exciting and fast paced. Great exercise. Run hard and enjoy it. Do it over and over, get a little dizzy and practice at the same time!

Peg

Number of kids: at least 2

Ages: 8 and up

Time allotted: at least 15 minutes

Space /Area: any driveway or concrete area with a wall at the end (best if the driveway or surface is on a downhill slant)

Equipment: one soft semi-bouncy ball (i.e. tennis ball) and a closed garage or wall

Description:

Startup: Players should form boundaries that include sidelines and a "pass line" at the end. The pass line should be about 10-15 feet down the driveway. The sidelines are usually the sides of the driveway. (With an area not on a driveway, simple mark makeshift lines with chalk, etc.) An order is then chosen and a line is formed behind the pass line accordingly.

Object: To peg others and to avoid being pegged.

Play: The first person in line takes the ball in hand and throws it against the garage. The next player in line must then catch the ball. That player then throws the ball against the wall for the next person. After one throws the ball, they must return to the back of the line.

There are two tricks to this game. The first is: for the throw to be legal, it must cross the designated pass line before it goes out of bounds across one of the sidelines. A player may, of course, catch the ball before it crosses the pass line. The second is: the player attempting to catch the ball must possess it before the ball goes past his or her body in any way.

If the ball is thrown illegally, so it goes out of bounds, the thrower must run and touch the wall and return across the pass line. During this run, the rest of the players try to grab the ball and peg the runner before that player returns across the pass line. If a legal throw goes past the catcher's body, the catcher must also make that same run. When the runner passes the crossline after touching the garage, the run is over and that player can no longer be pegged. The player who made the run simply gets in the end of line and whoever is then first in line gets the ball, and a new round begins.

There are several ways to end the game. Players may simply play continuously just for the thrill of playing. Players may also declare that if someone is hit, that player must sit out until the next round, and the winner is the last one standing. One other option is to play that a point is earned for being hit and a player is out when a certain number of points is reached.

Personal comments: A tad dangerous (so generally for older kids), but that is why this game is so fun. It you do not want to be hit with a ball, do not play. Do not throw towards heads or for the purpose of injuring someone. Aim low and just play for fun! Use good strategy and tricky throws. It is also important that during the game, you must be brave! Sometimes we used to let the ball go by on purpose just for the thrill of the run!

Red Devil[2]

Number of kids: at least 3

Ages: any

Time allotted: 20 minutes or more

Space /Area: a yard with a house or any large object to run around

Equipment: none

Description:

Startup: Players all begin in front of the house (or large object) and choose a "red devil".

Object: To be the red devil.

Play: The first red devil thinks of an object and the category to which it belongs (for example, "Snickers", and a category could be "candy bars"). The red devil then faces the other players and says "I am thinking of a type of….." (and names the category). The other players then take turns trying to guess what the red devil has thought of. When a correct answer is heard the red devil announces the name of the player who guessed it correctly. As soon as the name is said, that player and the red devil must run around the house as quickly as possible. The first person back becomes the red devil and a new round begins.

Option: For tired players or those who do not like to run, a rule can be used that says the first one back is *not* the red devil.

Personal Comments: May sound boring, but is actually a fun game. It is fun to think of tough categories as the red devil. Guessing and creativity, mixed with some short races, provides for a good time. Think hard and run fast!

Sardines

Number of kids: at least 4

Ages: any

Time allotted: 45 minutes or more

Space /Area: several connecting neighborhood yards (front and back) or a large area with places to hide

Equipment: none

Description:

Startup: Players should define boundaries and choose an "It".

Object: To find the It as soon as possible and to hide with him or her.

Play: Play begins as the It runs and hides. Everyone else counts to sixty with their eyes closed. Once sixty is reached, the players scatter to search for the It. If someone finds the It, instead of calling out, that player hides with the It. Plays continues until everyone has found the original It and has packed into the hiding place like sardines. Then the first player who found the original It is It for the next round. A time limit should be set of about 10 or 15 minutes in case someone cannot find the It's hiding spot. Player's can do as many rounds as desired.

Personal Comments: Best at night with flashlights!! The more people cramming into a hiding spot, the better. Pack in like sardines and have fun!

Slap the Nose[2]

Number of kids: at least 4

Ages: any

Time allotted: 1 hour or more

Space /Area: several connecting neighborhood yards (front and back) or a large area with places to hide

Equipment: none

Description:

Startup: Players should define boundaries, pick an "It", and choose a base (a wall or tree, etc.).

Object: To avoid being It.

Play: The person who is It hides his or her face against the base. Everyone else gathers behind the It. Someone draws a face on the It's back using his or her finger. The player describes what he or she is drawing ("here is the mouth", etc.). Anytime after the nose is drawn, any player, even the drawer, may slap the "nose". The object is to slap the nose so the It does not know who the slapper was. The It must then turn and identify who he or she thinks the culprit is. The accused player says "How far shall I run and how high shall I count?". The It then pronounces a distance, a direction, and a number. If the It has correctly identified the slapper, the slapper must run the distance and back while counting to the assigned number aloud. If the It was incorrect, then he or she must make the run.

Whoever is punished into running then becomes "It" for a game of hide and seek. While the punished runner is counting and running the assigned distance, everyone else runs and hides. After the distance is run and the number is counted, that person then begins to seek. The first person found is the It who will face the wall. Everyone else is called in and the next round begins. Players can do as many rounds as desired.

Personal Comments: Great game of accusation, punishment, sneakiness, and hide and seek. This is one that can be played for hours and should be!!

Spud

Number of kids: at least 4

Ages: any

Time allotted: at least 30 minutes

Space /Area: a large open yard or field

Equipment: one playground ball or other soft ball

Description:

Startup: There are no real boundaries, just a nice open area. Once players select a ball and an area, everyone counts off a number, 1 thru "x" (x being the number of kids playing), so that each player has their own individual number.

Object: Not to gain the letters S...P...U...D.

Play: One player starts with the ball and everyone gathers in a circle. The player with the ball, throws it straight into the air and calls out a player's number (1 thru "x"). All players may begin to spread anywhere as soon as the ball is tossed. Whoever's number is called (and only that player) must catch the ball as soon as possible. When the ball is caught by this player, he or she yells "Freeze!". All other players must stop immediately where they are. The player with the ball may then take two large hops in any direction. This player then attempts to hit another player with the ball. The other player may dodge the ball, but cannot move until the ball is thrown. If the ball hits the other player before touching the ground, the player hit receives the letter "S". If an "S" has already been received by this player, then a "P" is given, then "U", then "D". If the player with the ball fails to hit someone on the throw attempt, he or she receives a letter. Everyone then comes back together and the player who received a letter gets to toss up the ball and call out the next number, and the entire process repeats. The game ends when on player spells SPUD. The winner(s) are the players with the fewest letters. Start a new round.

Personal comments: Another childhood top five!! Sounds strange but worth a try! This can really grow on kids and can be very exciting for everyone. Whether yelling a number, dodging, or watching another player being hit, you will have a blast!

Variant: Buddy Spud: Play with teams of two. When your team's number is called, either player can go for the ball, the teammate should run amongst the other players. After "Freeze!" is called, everyone must stop, even the teammate of the person who called "Freeze!". The ball may then be thrown as described above, or it may be passed to the teammate. Either play may take the hops, but only two total jumps are allowed. Only one pass is allowed. A pass must also be caught successfully a letter is earned. Each player of a team earns letters together, not separately. All other rules stand.

Variant: Call Ball[1]: In this game, players do not spread when the ball is thrown. Instead, the game only consists of the initial toss. The player tossing the ball is the "It". The It tosses the ball straight up and the player who is called must catch the ball in the air. If the player does not catch it, he or she becomes It, and if the ball is caught, the It remains It and must toss again.

Stoop Ball

Number of kids: at least 2

Ages: any

Time allotted: 20 minutes or more

Space /Area: an open street in front of a building with steps

Equipment: one bouncy ball, such as a racquet ball

Description:

Startup: Players should find a good location, split into two teams, and define the throwing line. One team begins in the field and the other is up to bat, or one on one can be played (see *options* 3 and 4 below).

Object: To score the most runs.

Play: The first player up to bat stands behind the throwing line, faces the building, and throws the ball against the steps as hard as he or she desires. The ball must then strike the steps and ricochet back into the street. The ball must travel in the air at least passed the throwing line. Rules similar to baseball then follow. If the ball misses the steps or fails to ricochet passed the throwing line, the batter receives a strike. Three strikes and the batter is out. If the ball does ricochet passed the throwing line, it is in play. This is where several variations have emerged, each is explained in *options* below.

Options: 1. When a ball is in play, the batter is out if the ball is caught in the air by an opponent. If the ball bounces once before a catch, the batter receives a single (as in baseball). If the ball bounces twice, a double is earned, and a triple is earned for three bounces, and a home run is earned for four of more bounces. Ghost runners (pretend) should be used in lue of actual base running. Batters continue to switch and bat until three outs are earned, then the teams switch. Play any number of innings or up to a certain score.

    2. When a ball is in play, the number of bases received can be determined strictly by how far the ball travels before it lands. Lines can be marked before the game to indicate a single, double, triple, or home run. Again, the batter is out if three strikes are received or if an opponent catches the ball in the air.

    3. For one-on-one play, option 2 can be followed with one rule change. Instead of strikes, outs are received for throws not in play.

    4. Another one-on-one option is to award a single if the fielder cannot stop the ball cleanly, a double if the ball passes the fielder, and a home run if the ball flies over the fielder's head. For this, a line where the fielder should stand should be marked. Outs are issued if a defender can catch or cleanly stop the ball before it passes him or her, and also for throws not in play.

Personal Comments: A classic game that seems more popular in big cities, but can be played anywhere. Perfecting the throw is the hardest part of the game, but practicing and playing are non-stop excitement. Find a good area to play and try this out!

Swat Tag[4]

Number of kids: at least 4

Ages: any

Time allotted: 10 minutes or more

Space /Area: any open area

Equipment: one rolled up newspaper

Description:

Startup: Players should choose an "It". Everyone else gets into a circle facing counterclockwise with their hands behind their backs. Players must turn so that they are facing the person's back in front of them and must keep their eyes on the back of that player.

Object: To swat the other players as much as possible.

Play: The person chosen as It walks around the outside of the circle and places the newspaper into the hands of one of the other players. This player becomes the "swatter" and instantly smacks the player in front of him or her below the waist with the newspaper. The person in front then becomes the "runner". The swatter then chases the runner around the circle hitting the runner as many times as possible below the waist before the runner returns to his or her original position. The runner then becomes the new It, everyone else gets into a circle again, and the process starts over. The former swatter and It have rejoined the circle. Plays continues until players simply decide to stop.

Personal Comments: Do not play if you do not want to be hit on the rear with a newspaper. This can be really funny to watch and play. It's good to take out some innocent aggression and to watch your friends get swatted. It really does not hurt to get swatted, but is still a ton of fun to go swat someone!!

Ten Ball

Number of kids: at least 2

Ages: any

Time allotted: 20 minutes or more

Space /Area: any large wall with a paved area in front

Equipment: a semi-bouncy ball such as a tennis ball

Description:

Startup: Players should find a wall to use and choose an order of players.

Object: To complete all 10 challenges.

Play: The first player begins with the ball and creates the first challenge. The challenge must include tossing the ball against the wall and catching it in the air or after one bounce. For example, "the player must hike the ball against the wall, turn around, and catch it in the air". Each player must then complete this challenge while saying "one ball". The next player then creates a different challenge. Players then must perform the first challenge while saying "one ball", then perform the second challenge while saying "two ball". The next player then adds the third challenge and the process repeats. Every round, each player must perform each challenge in order, starting with the first. This should continue until ten challenges have been created and performed. If a player does not complete any challenge correctly, he or she is eliminated from the game. Play continues until only one player is left or until 10 challenges are completed. In the latter case, all players completing the 10 challenges win.

Personal comments: Creating the challenges is the best part of this game! Really be creative and out do your opponents. Make difficult challenges, but remember you have to complete them as well as everyone else. Practice specialty tosses between games to help you win. It is a blast to watch your friends try all the crazy tricks and to try them yourself!

What's the Time Mr. Wolf?[2]

Number of kids: 3 or more

Ages: any

Time allotted: 20 minutes or more

Space /Area: any decent sized safe area

Equipment: none

Description:

Startup: Players pick one person to be the "wolf". Everyone else lines up about 20 feet behind the wolf. The wolf then faces away from the other players.

Object: To get close to the wolf and not get caught.

Play: When everyone is set, the group calls out "What's the time Mr. Wolf?". The wolf then turns to the others and calls out a time (for example, 5 o'clock) and turns back around. The players then take that many steps towards the wolf (so if the wolf did say 5 o'clock, 5 steps would be taken, and for 12 o'clock, 12 steps would be taken, etc.). The wolf may only look at the group when announcing the time. The group then again asks "What's the time Mr. Wolf?" the wolf responds, and the group moves accordingly. This continues until the wolf senses the group is close, then instead of calling a number, the wolf says "DINNER TIME!" and runs after all the other players. Whoever is caught by the wolf before getting back to the starting line is the next wolf. If no one is caught, the last person back to the finish line, besides the wolf, is the next wolf. Players can do as many round as desired.

Personal Comments: Good for some startles. Be sneaky as the wolf. Do not wait until they get too close, or else it is no fun, but try to take the players off guard and grab someone quick. As players, try to get close to the wolf, do not hide in the back. Be risky and have fun!

Activity Level II

500

Number of kids: at least 4

Ages: any

Time allotted: 20 minutes or more

Space /Area: a long strip of grass or pavement

Equipment: one soft football (other types of balls may be substituted, but footballs are best)

Description:

Startup: Player should select a ball and choose one person to be the thrower.

Object: To become the thrower by earning 500 points.

Play: The thrower lines up away from everyone else roughly the distance he or she can easily toss the football. Everyone else stand near each other. When everyone is set, the thrower chooses a number of points, for example, 200. The thrower then yells this number to everyone and at the same time, throws the ball into the air. The ball should land somewhere amongst the group of catchers. If a player catches the ball, that player earns the number of points called by the thrower. In this example, the catcher would get 200 points for catching the ball in the air. A generally accepted *option* is also awarding half the points for catching the ball after one bounce (so 100 points would be earned on a 200 point throw if the ball bounces one time). If no one catches the ball, no points are earned. Either way, the ball is then returned to the thrower, who again calls out a chosen number while throwing the football. Once a catcher reaches a point total of 500 or more, that player then becomes the thrower and another round begins. Every time a new player becomes the thrower, everyone's point totals reset to zero. Play ends when the players no longer wish to play.

Options: Two non-standard calls exist and may be used by the thrower if desired. "Jackpot" may be called, meaning an automatic token to 500 for anyone who catches the ball (only applies if caught in the air). "Mystery" may also be called, where only the thrower knows the value of the toss until it is caught (one bounce is still acceptable for half points here, unless of course the mystery is a Jackpot!).

Personal comments: This is a fun game that anyone can play. The trick is to have fun throwing. Throw some high, some low, some a little off to the side, some real far or short. Mix up the calls too, and do not be too stingy. Really be aggressive in catching as well, but be careful not to mow over smaller players! Fun to watch and play, give it a shot!

Attack[3]

Number of kids: 2 teams of at least 3

Ages: 8 and up

Time allotted: 20 minutes or more

Space /Area: any open grassy area

Equipment: none

Description:

Startup: Players should split into two teams and define a circular area to be the region of "attack". The circle should include a line across the middle, called the "pull line". Players on each team should choose a captain.

Object: To be on the team that scores the most points.

Play: One captain chooses a player from each team to "attack" in the circle. The other captain then chooses the method of the attack**. The two chosen players enter the circle, do battle, and a point is given to the winner. This process repeats after each attack except the captains alternate jobs. This goes until one team has reached a predetermined number of wins.

   **Methods of attack include (but are not limited to):
1. Grasp right hands (or left hands) over the pull line and try to pull opponent over the line.
2. Link right elbows (or left elbows) over the pull line and pull opponent over the line.
3. Break through opponent's line first. The players of the two teams join hands standing on their own side of the circle. The attackers then try to be the first to break through their opponent's line.
4. Fold arms across chest and push opponent out of the combat circle.
5. Hop on one foot, holding the other foot behind the body in one hand, and with the other arm across the chest and grasping the opposite shoulder, cause opponent to replace his foot to the floor or fall over.
6. One player must run to a chosen spot before the opponent tags him or her (a slight lead is given to the runner).
7. To be the first to knock off, or steal the opponent's hat without stepping outside the circle.
8. To be the first to snatch the opponent's tail without stepping outside the circle. For this, a handkerchief or cloth band is placed under the back of each player's belt or waistline.

Personal Comments: Try these rules, but make up some more and have fun doing it. Try to pick some even battles and some fun lopsided ones. Use good strategy in picking players and attacks, but give everyone a chance! Go try hard and it will be a blast!

Buck, Buck[1]

Number of kids: 2 teams of at least 4

Ages: 8 and up

Time allotted: 20 minutes or more

Space /Area: an open grass area

Equipment: none

Description:

Startup: Players should find an open place to play and choose teams. One teams decides to be the "buck" and the other team is the "jumpers". One player on the buck's team stands up straight and is called the "post". Another player on the buck's team then bends over and braces himself or herself against the post. The rest of that team continues this trend, each bending over and wrapping their arms around the player's waist in front of them, forming the buck. The post should be facing the same direction as the rest of his or her team. The jumpers all stand about 10 feet behind the end of the buck.

Object: To collapse the buck.

Play: The first jumper holds up 1, 2, or 3 fingers and yells "Buck, buck, how many fingers do I hold up?". The post cannot look and must guess 1, 2, or 3. If the post is correct, that jumper's turn is over and the next jumper does the same. If the post is wrong, the jumper replies, "3 you say, and 2 there be" (substitute the appropriate numbers). The jumper is then allowed to run and leap (from behind) onto the buck. The jumper should leap as far as he or she can to allow room for others. A jumper should land by straddling the buck, as one would sit on a horse. The next jumper then repeats the entire process. Each jumper gets one turn and the round ends. During this round, jumpers are trying to collapse the buck. If successful, the jumpers earn one point, and if unsuccessful, the buck earns one point. The teams then switch and the process repeats. The winner is the team that accumulates the most points at the end of several rounds.

Personal comments: This game is a riot. It does get physical and there is risk of injury, so be careful. Do not play if you do not want to be jumped on. Otherwise, this game is fantastic. It is challenging and non-stop excitement. There is a lot of strategy in determining the order of jumpers and in forming the buck. Be careful, but play this game to its fullest!

Crossing the Brook[1]

Number of kids: at least 2

Ages: any

Time allotted: 5 minutes or more

Space /Area: any open grass area

Equipment: two objects to mark the ends of the "brook" (broom sticks, pieces of rope, etc.)

Description:

Startup: Place the two chosen objects a few feet apart.

Object: To be the last remaining player.

Play: Players take turns attempting to jump over the "brook". Each player who does not successfully jump all the way across the brook is eliminated from the game. After each player has jumped, the brook is widened and the remaining players must jump it again. Each round, the brook is widened until only one player successfully jumps over it. This player is the winner.

Personal comments: A good game to test your leaping skills. Widen it slowly to add excitement. It is fun to watch everyone try to fly over the brook and to see just how far you can fly.

Exchange[3]

Number of kids: 7 or more

Ages: any (better for younger kids)

Time allotted: 15 minutes or more

Space /Area: any small, open area

Equipment: none

Description:

Startup: Players choose an "It" and everyone else gathers around the It in a circle.

Object: To avoid being It.

Play: The It calls out the names of two players in the circle. These players then attempt to switch places. At the same time, the It is trying to jump into one of their places in the circle. The It must start in the middle of the circle and no one can move until both names are called. Whoever does not get one of the two open spots is the It for the next round. Play continues until players decide to stop.

Option: Everyone can make up a funny name and those can be used.

Personal Comments: Super easy game. One that a group of younger kids can play almost anytime. Try it out!

Four Square

Number of kids: 4 or more

Ages: any

Time allotted: at least 30 minutes

Space /Area: a driveway with large squares or pavement with drawn squares

Equipment: one playground ball or basketball

Description:

Startup: Players should choose a ball and find a driveway that is divided into squares, or draw large squares on the pavement in a safe location. Each player is assigned a square. If there are too many players, the others form a line outside the squares and will rotate into play. Designate squares as "A", "B", "C", "D", and perhaps "E" and "F" if there are enough players and 6 six squares are desired.

Object: To be in the "A" square.

Play: Everyone gets into their assigned square. At no time may a player go into someone else's square, unless diving to save the ball. The person in the "A" square begins with the ball and gets to make the rules** at the beginning of each point. That player then serves the ball to another square. If the ball lands in a player's square, that player must hit the ball into another square safely and legally. A player must hit or catch the ball (depending on the rules) before it lands or after one bounce, but cannot leave his or her square to do so (unless going for a save). A point continues until one person gets out. If the player does not touch the ball or does so illegally, he or she is out. If, at any time, the ball bounces twice before a player can get to it, that player is out. If a player breaks the rules (designated by the server in "A") while handling it, that player is out. If a player hits the ball out of bounds or into his or her own square, that player is out.

If for any of these reason a player gets out, he or she must go to the last square or to the back of the line. Everyone then moves up one square accordingly (for example, if "B" gets out, "C" moves to "B", "D" moves to "C", etc.). As long as the same person is in "A", the rules do not change. As soon as a new person takes the "A" square, that player makes his or her own rules. Play continues until the players are ready to stop.

If no special rules are desired by the "A" square, "clean" play constitutes only bumping the ball into another square. This rule means: no catching, clean serves, only one bounce, no hitting the balls into the corners, no spikes, etc. This can be called by saying "clean".

**The rules for each point are generally chosen from this list of options. The person in the "A" square picks as many as he or she would like or can create his or her own:

Catching: one is allowed to catch the ball, carry it, and throw it.
Bobbles: instead of catching the ball, one is allowed to bobble it up and down temporarily.
Shoe shiners: one may never peg another person, but this rule allows the ball to be thrown against another's shoe to get them out.
Sky scrapers: this is when the ball is slammed down in another's square, so that it bounces high and far to get someone out.
Corners: this allows one to hit dirty shots into the corners of another's square.
Fast throw: this allows for hard hits or fast throws (only effective when catching is allowed).
Spins: one can put crazy spins on the ball to make it harder for another to catch (only truly effective when catching is allowed).
Dirty serves: allows the "A" player to serve the ball using a special rule.
Around the world: Each player must hit the ball into the square immediately lower than theirs (A to B, B to C, etc.). If the ball gets to the lowest square, he or she must hit it back to the "A" square, and so forth.
Doubles: temporary pairs (such as A with B and C with D) can be made to play as teams.
Create a rule: use only left hand, etc.

Personal comments: Perhaps my favorite childhood game. With all the rule variations and constant bloopers, this is a riot. Go get a bunch of people, play for a long time. Be competitive and have fun mixing up the rules.

Variant: Paddle Four Square

This games uses the same rules with paddles. In this version, be careful players are far enough apart they do not risk hitting each other!

Variant: Two Square

All the same rules can apply with simply two people. In this game, players should take turns serving and should play to a certain number of points, such as 10.

Garage Ball Tag

Number of kids: at least 3

Ages: any

Time allotted: 15 minutes or more

Space /Area: a garage or an open wall

Equipment: one soft ball

Description:

Startup: Players should select a ball and find a good wall to use. Players should also define boundaries against the wall that include side boundaries and a line about 20 feet back from that wall. Then players choose an "It".

Object: To avoid being It.

Play: Once an It is chosen, everyone else gets against the garage and spreads out as desired within the defined boundaries. The It must stand behind the chosen line and attempt to hit other players with the ball. If a throw is missed, the It retrieves the ball, again gets behind the line, and tries again. If the It is successful in hitting another player with the ball, that player becomes the It and play continues. Players may run and dodge the ball in any way they choose, as long as they stay against the wall. Players may also catch the ball to avoid becoming It. If the ball is caught, it is tossed back to the It and play continues. The game continues until the players desire to stop.

Personal comments: This is even more fun that it sounds. When you are against a wall, it is harder to dodge a ball than you might imagine. It is better to have narrow boundaries and be crowded together against the wall to make dodging more difficult.

Hand Slap[4]

Number of kids: 2 or more

Ages: 8 and up

Time allotted: 15 minutes or more

Space /Area: a small open area

Equipment: one 2 x 4 or a long flat log

Description:

Startup: Player should set the 2 x 4 or log on the ground and stand on top of it with one foot in front of the other.

Object: To knock the other player off the board.

Play: While on the board, players extend their hands and touch palms. As soon as the palms touch, the game begins. The players then try to knock each other off by slapping hands. Players must keep both palms facing the other player. No part of the body can be struck except the hand. The last one standing on the board is the winner. If both players fall off, it is a draw.

Personal Comments: Good for quick competition and balance practice. Fun to watch and play, but be careful only to slap palms and not to hurt the other player in any way. Mix up your strategy and enjoy the action!

Hide and Seek

Number of kids: at least 4

Ages: any

Time allotted: 45 minutes or more

Space /Area: several connecting neighborhood yards (front and back) or a large area with places to hide

Equipment: none

Description:

Startup: Players should define boundaries and choose an "It".

Object: To avoid being It.

Play: The It begins by counting to 60, while everyone else runs and hides. After counting the 60, the It should announce "Ready or not, here I come!". The It should then begin to search for everyone who is hiding. The first person found will be It for the next round. When a player is found, call everyone else to come out of hiding and play again.

Personal Comments: This game is a classic, simple as can be, and an absolute blast. That is why it has been around for so long. A must know and play for all kids! Hide well!

Hopscotch

Number of kids: at least 2

Ages: any

Time allotted: 20 minutes or more

Space /Area: any safe pavement or sidewalk where chalk drawings can be made

Equipment: a rock for each player and one piece of chalk

Description:

Startup: Players should draw a series of boxes on the pavement using a piece of chalk. These boxes need to be connected and can be one or two boxes wide. They should also be numbered, counting up from 1, with box 1 being the closest to the starting line. After the boxes are drawn, players choose an order.

Object: To score the most points or to finish first.

Play: The first player tosses his or her rock onto the series of boxes. Observe the number of the box where the rock landed. This is the number of points the player will get for a successful run. A successful run is made by getting to the rock, picking it up, and getting back across the starting line without messing up. The trick is that each box along the way can only be stepped in once. For a single box, only one foot can be used. If the boxes are two wide, two feet may be used (one in each box), or each must be landed in sequentially with one foot (depending on the predetermined rules). If a player can follow the stepping pattern, bend over and pick up the rock, and skip back to the start (in the same fashion) without messing up or falling down, that player earns the number of points in the box where his or her rock was laying. The winner is the first to a predetermined number of points or whoever has the highest point total after so many rounds.

Another version of play can be used where each player must make a successful run in each box, starting with 1 and ending with the highest number. The first player must make a successful run after landing his or her rock in box 1, then box 2, and so on. A player continues until he or she makes a mistake or throws the rock into the wrong box. The next round that player will continue on the box where he or she made the mistake in the previous round. The first person successful in completing each box is the winner.

Personal Comments: A classic good for younger kids. If you have never tried this game, give it a shot.

Indian Wrestling

Number of kids: 2, but can be done with more

Ages: any

Time allotted: 10 minutes or more

Space /Area: any semi-soft ground area, such as grass

Equipment: none

Description:

Startup: Whoever wishes to wrestle "lines up" within the selected area. Players line up by sitting down hip to hip, facing opposite directions. Players then lay back so they are still lying in opposite directions (so a player's head is roughly next to the other players heel). The players' hips should still be touching.

Object: To push the opponent over into a back somersault.

Play: Once lined up, a start similar to a face-off occurs. Each player's inside leg is raised so that the opponents' feet touch. They then lower their legs back to the ground. This is done twice. At the third leg raise, both opponents pull their inside leg back a little further so they can hook each other's legs between the foot and knee. The wrestlers then use leverage to try to lower their leg, forcing the opponent's body to roll over backwards. The winner, of course, is the one who pushes over the other.

Variant: The wrestlers should stand up and line up one foot (right to right, or left to left) toe-to-toe and grab wrists (of the same side of the body as the aligned foot). Players should put the other leg behind them for support. The wrestlers then count to three and say "Go!". The goal is then to try to pull the opponent over the middle. The winner is the wrestler who successfully pulls the opponent over the middle.

Personal comments: These are easy but fun games to brag about and enjoyable to watch! They are quite different than most other competitions. It is a great time coming up with unique strategies. Grab an opponent and see how you do!

Log Roll[1]

Number of kids: at least 2

Ages: any

Time allotted: 10 minutes or more

Space /Area: any open grass area

Equipment: one log

Description:

Startup: Players should find a good, round log and an open area to set it. Each player then steps up on top of the log.

Object: To be the last player on the log.

Play: One player yells "Ready, set, go!" and the game begins. Players then try to shake the other players off the log by rocking the log back and forth. Physical contact is not allowed, but anything else goes. If a player touches the ground in any way, this player is eliminated and must walk away from the log. Play continues until only one player is left on the log. This player is the winner.

Personal comments: A very simple game, but amazingly fun. Staying on a log with 2 or 3 people trying to roll it is much harder than you might think. Flying off and watching everyone else get sent off the log are great for some laughs. Test your balance, try different rolling techniques, and stay on the log!

Monkey in the Middle (also called: Keep Away)

Number of kids: 3 or more

Ages: any

Time allotted: 10 minutes or more

Space /Area: any decent sized open area

Equipment: any object(s) that can be easily carried and passed

Description:

Startup: Players should set boundaries and choose the "monkey" (or monkeys if there are enough people) to be in the middle. There should be one object to be tossed per monkey.

Object: To avoid being the monkey.

Play: Everyone circles around the monkey and tosses the object back and forth. The monkey then tries to steal the object from the other players while it is in the air or on the ground. The monkey cannot take the object out of someone else's hands, but may do anything else (non-physical) to get the object. If the monkey does gain possession of the object, the person responsible takes the monkey's place and the game continues. The game ends when players feel like stopping.

Personal Comments: This is one everyone may already know, but it is a classic and is still fun.

Palm Boxing[4]

Number of kids: 2 (more than 2 can simply take turns)

Ages: 8 and up

Time allotted: 10 minutes or more

Space /Area: a small open area

Equipment: none

Description:

Startup: The two players stand close together. Players should face each other and push their own heels together.

Object: To knock the other player off balance.

Play: When in position, the opponents then reach out and put their palms together. As soon as the palms touch, the round begins. Keeping their palms against each other's, boxers try to push each other off balance by pushing with one or both hands. Players can move their bodies around, dodging, etc., but may not move their feet. The first player to move of lift his toes or heels is the loser.

Personal Comments: This is a game where the little guy can actually win. Dodging, body movement, and pushing on and off with the arms can be used for strategy, not just power. This is a game that takes more talent than it seems. Practice and get good and this can be a ton of fun!!

Poison Circle[3]

Number of kids: 2 teams of at least 2

Ages: 8 and up

Time allotted: 25 minutes or more

Space /Area: an open grassy area

Equipment: anything to mark a circle

Description:

Startup: Teams are chosen and a circle is drawn or marked on the grass. The team should spread out around the outside of the circle. Each player should have an opponent on each side. Everyone joins hands.

Object: To be on the team with the surviving players.

Play: The game begins as one player yells "Ready, set, go!". Everyone then tries to pull their opponents into the circle without stepping in the circle themselves. As soon as one person steps in the circle, play instantly stops (so that only one player may get eliminated at a time). The player who stepped in the circle first is eliminated. Hands are held once again, forming a new circle, and a new round ensues. If the circle needs to shrink, create a new one as necessary. The team who has the last remaining player(s) is the winner.

Personal Comments: This is a fantastic version of tug-of-war. It's fun and chaotic. It may get messy, but is fun to watch everyone pull and fall. Try leaning back as well as pulling forward, Finding the right balance is tougher than it sounds. Play hard and don't be afraid to get a little physical with this game.

Prisoner's Attack[3]

Number of kids: 2 teams of at least 3

Ages: any

Time allotted: 30 minutes or more

Space /Area: any large open grassy area or field

Equipment: one ball

Description:

Startup: Players should define boundaries that include two even sized rectangular or circular playing areas with a large neutral area in between them. Boundaries also include a prison area behind each playing area. Players should then choose teams and have one team go to each playing area.

Object: To imprison all of the opponents.

Play: One team starts with the ball. They may pass it amongst themselves or throw it towards the other team's playing area. When a player throws the ball towards the other playing area, he or she must call out an opponent's name AS THE BALL IS THROWN. Someone on the other team must then catch the ball before it lands within their playing area. If a catch is not made and the ball lands in the playing area, the player whose name was called must go to the other team's prison. The other team then throws the ball back in the same fashion. If the ball lands in the neutral territory or anywhere out of bounds, the throw is wasted and the other team gets the ball. Teams throw the ball back and forth until all the players on one team are imprisoned.

Players may get out of prison if a bad throw lands in their prison area. They can then pick up the ball and try to hit a player on the other team with the ball. The ball must hit the other player in the air without being caught. If successful, the prisoner may return to his or her playing area.

Play always stops when a player is entering or leaving jail. The ball always switches possession after each throw. If a prisoner attempts to free himself (successfully or unsuccessfully) the ball goes to the other team afterwards. Once a team has imprisoned everyone on the other team, the game is over and that team wins.

Personal Comments: A challenging game. It sounds complicated, but is very easy to play and goes smoothly after a couple practice rounds. Play fair and do not simply whiz the ball. Try for placement and passing strategy. Good for throwing, catching, and team skills are required. This game is a lot different from most and is fun for all!

Variant: Play every man for himself. Each player gets a little playing area of his or her own, and is eliminated instead of going to prison. If a player eliminates someone, he or she gets the ball back.

Red Rover

Number of kids: 2 teams of at least 4

Ages: any

Time allotted: 30 minutes or more

Space /Area: a good sized yard or grassy area

Equipment: none

Description:

Startup: Players choose two teams. Each team gets in a side-by-side line, one team facing the other, about 10 yards apart. Each player grabs the wrist or hand of each person next to them.

Object: To capture each opponent.

Play: One team is chosen to go first. They confer and decide on a player from the other team to challenge. Everyone on the challenging team says "Red rover, red rover, send [player's name] over". The player called then leaves his or her line and charges towards the challenging team's line. The challenged player must try to break through the opponent's line by charging BETWEEN (not over) two players, breaking their arms apart. If he or she cannot break the chain, that player is then captured, and must join the chain where he or she failed to break it. If the challenged player does successfully break the chain, that player gets to return to his or her original line. He or she also gets to bring back one of the two players where the chain broke. After this process, the other team then calls a player and the process repeats. The teams go back and forth until one team is the clear winner. This is usually when only one or two players are left on a side. One option can be that when one player is left, he or she has one last chance to break the opponent's chain, or it is over. Once the game is over, form new teams and play again.

Personal Comments: A classic game. Fun to play, especially with a large number of kids. Good competition and fun for some laughs. Be strategic about who to call and where to run when called, but no matter what, really try to bust through the line!

Treasure Hunt

Number of kids: 2 or more

Ages: any

Time allotted: 45 minutes or more

Space /Area: anywhere safe

Equipment: one or more treasures to find and materials to make clues

Description:

Startup: One child or adult must form the hunt. This includes making and hiding a series of clues for the other players to follow, and hiding the final treasure(s).

Object: To successfully decipher the clues in order to find the treasure.

Play: After the hunt designer has made and hidden all the clues and the treasure, the others players are called to begin. They are given the first clue at the designated starting point and the hunt begins. Of course, the game ends when the players successfully solve all the clues and end up finding the treasure. Take turns creating the hunts.

Personal Comments: This is a fun game, especially with good creative clues. Long, tough hunt they are often more fun. Be creative with the clues and go enjoy it.

Variant: Instead of forming clues, one player simply hides a series of objects in a given area and the winner is the player who finds the most.

Tug of War

Number of kids: 2 teams of at least 2

Ages: any

Time allotted: 10 minutes or more

Space /Area: any open strip of ground

Equipment: one long thick rope

Description:

Startup: Players should find a long thick rope, define a middle line, and choose teams. Teams should separate, with one team on each side of the middle line. Make sure exactly half of the rope lies on each side of the middle line. Everyone picks up the rope and braces themselves.

Object: To pull the front person of the other team over the middle line.

Play: Once everyone has a good hold of the rope, one player say "ready, set, pull!" and both teams begin to pull. Play continues until one of the men closest to the middle line is pulled over the line. The team who pulls the other man over the middle line is the winner.

Personal comments: This is a fun and easy game. It's a classic, but a must-play!

Activity Level I

Around the World

Number of kids: at least 2

Ages: any

Time allotted: 30 minutes or more

Space /Area: any basketball area

Equipment: one basketball

Description:

Startup: Players should find an area to play and choose a shooting order. Everyone should then determine a series of shots that must be made to complete a round. Usually 3 paths are used that require 5 shot each (one shot from one side, then the corner, then from straight on, then from the other corner, then the other side). The first path should be the smallest, then one a little farther away, then one around the 3-point range.

Object: To get "around the world" by making every designated shot.

Play: The first player starts with the ball and begins the series of shots. If the first shot is made, that player immediately advanced to the next shot and continues. If that player finishes one ring, he or she immediately continues to the first shot on the next ring. If the player should miss a shot, "chances" come into play. If a player misses, that player may simply decide to stay in place until the next turn or he or she can take a "chance". Two chances are possible. If a player takes the first chance, that player may shoot again. If he or she makes the shot on the first "chance", that player moves to the next shot and his or her turn continues, as before. If the "chance" is missed, that player must restart at the very beginning at his or her next turn. The second "chance" is an optional rule. This may be taken, and results in an automatic elimination from the game instead of the returning to the beginning. Play ends when one player makes it all the way "around the world".

Personal comments: This is more competitive for decent basketball players, but can be played by anyone. The second chance rule should only be played by beginners and if there is a lot of people. With skilled players, two chances makes it too easy to go all the way around in one turn. Overall this is a good, skillful game.

Bean Bag Toss

Number of kids: at least 2

Ages: any

Time allotted: 20 minutes or more

Space /Area: any open area

Equipment: At least 3 bean bags and the playing board. The playing board can be made of any large, flat, rectangular board. Holes that the bean bags can fit through should be cut in the board (where and how many can vary as desired). This board can be propped up against a wall, or back legs can be built to angle it.

Description:

Startup: Once the playing board is made and a location is found, players should assign point values to each hole in the board. A throwing line should also be marked about 20 feet away from the board.

Object: To score the highest number of points.

Play: Each player stands behind the throwing line and takes turns tossing three bean bags towards the board. If a bean bag goes through a hole in the board, that player scores the corresponding number of points. Each player totals his or her points at the end of each round. The winner is the first player to reach a certain number of points (determined before the game). A determined number of rounds may also be played, in which case the player with the highest total at the end of the last round is the winner.

Personal Comments: A childhood favorite, especially when I was younger. Making and decorating the board can be a fun project to do as parent and child. We used to make clown faces with holes in the eyes, nose, and mouth, but anything goes, so be creative and have fun. This is a fun simple game that anyone can play!

Bocce

Number of kids: at least 2

Ages: any

Time allotted: 20 minutes or more

Space /Area: any large grassy area

Equipment: one small ball (the "bocce") and 2 or 3 slightly larger ones for each child (for example, one golf ball and several tennis balls for each child)

Description:

Startup: Players should choose the balls and find a good area to play.

Object: To toss one's balls closest to the bocce.

Play: One player tosses the smaller "bocce" ball as far as he or she desires. Everyone else then takes turns tossing one of their balls towards the bocce ball. Once everyone has tossed once, everyone tosses a second time, and so on, until all balls have been tossed. Whichever player lands one of their balls closest to the bocce is the winner. The winner then tosses the bocce for the next round. Play one round at a time or a series that continues until one player has 5 or 10 wins.

Personal comments: Seems corny and simply, but is actually a ton of fun. It takes more skill than you might imagine. Vary how far you throw the bocce and give this game a shot!

Building (dam, fort, tree house, etc.)

Number of kids: 1 or more

Ages: 8 and up

Time allotted: at least one hour

Space /Area: anywhere safe

Equipment: anything safe (for child to decide with possible supervision)

Description:

Startup: The players should choose an object to build and a safe area in which to build it.

Object: To finish whatever is chosen.

Play: Anything safe goes. Builders should find things to use and try to put them together as needed. The goal should be to make something stable or useful (perhaps to walk across, sit in, or play with). Keep trying new building ideas and techniques until whatever works best is discovered.

Personal comments: All this takes is creativity. Be creative not only in what you decide to build, but what you use to build it!! You just have to get outside and go for it. Pick long term projects. The longer and harder it is to build the dam, fort, or object, the more rewarding it is when you finish. Do not be afraid to get a little dirty too!

Circle Target Bowl[3]

Number of kids: at least 2

Ages: any

Time allotted: 30 minutes or more

Space /Area: an open strip of short grass

Equipment: something to mark 3 concentric circles and one or more balls to roll for each child

Description:

Startup: Players should mark off 3 or more concentric circles and assign points value to each. The values should be assigned by giving the innermost circle the highest value with values decreasing towards the outside. Players then designate a starting line, a reasonable distance from the circles, any may choose teams if desired.

Object: To score the most points.

Play: Each player stands behind the starting line and takes turns rolling their ball(s) towards the circles. Each player must roll from behind the starting line. After all the balls have been rolled, the players or teams tally up the points they have earned. The winner can be the first to reach a set number of points or whoever has the highest total after 10 rounds.

Personal Comments: Good with teams and with kids of all ages. The older you are, the farther back the starting line should be and the smaller the circles should be. Super easy and super fun! Try this one out.

Variant: Multiple Target Throw[3]: This game is played by throwing objects (player's choice) instead of bowling. Players can use concentric circles, one lone target, or multiple targets. If multiple targets are used, targets should be close to each other and the smaller targets should be worth more points. Targets can also be changed between rounds if desired.

Personal Comments: Be creative with this. You can play in the sand or in the snow or in the mud (if you want to get dirty), or just use chalk or cones. Vary the circle sizes or move them around. Go out, explore the possibilities, and enjoy it.

Cornhole

Number of kids: 2 teams of 2

Ages: any

Time allotted: 40 minutes or more

Space /Area: any long open area

Equipment: Eight bean bags: two matching sets of four.
Two slightly slanted bean bag boards. These can be made using thin plywood. The boards should be about 2 feet wide, 4 feet long, and the back end should be raised about one foot. They should only have one hole in the middle upper part of the board, big enough for the bean bag to fall through.

Description:

Startup: Players should spread the two boards about 20 feet apart. Two players, one from each team, then stand beside each board. One's partner should then be standing at the opposing board, with one opponent at each board. All eight beanbags start on one side and one set goes to each player.

Object: To score 21 points first.

Play: The players with the bags take turns tossing one bean bag towards the opposite board until all bags are tossed. Players are not allowed to cross the front of their board while tossing. At the end of that round, one point is earned by a team for each of their bags that is on top of the board and three points are awarded for each bag that fell through the hole. Here is the tricky part: only the difference in score is kept (so if team A scores 8 points and team B scores 5, team A gets 3 points for that round and team B gets nothing). After the final points are tallied, the other two players then toss the bags in the same fashion. The team that has most recently gained points throws the first bag. The game ends when 21 points are reached.

Personal Comments: This is a slightly more complicated than a regular bean bag toss, but is much more fun for older kids and even parents. This takes a lot of skill. Play for awhile and get good, close competition makes the game even more fun!

Deadbox[2]

Number of kids: at least 2

Ages: any

Time allotted: 45 minutes or more

Space /Area: a safe area of pavement or cement that can be drawn on by chalk

Equipment: chalk and one metal bottle cap for each player

Description:

Startup: One player should draw a large box on the ground with the chalk. Within the box, ten smaller boxes along the inside edge should be draw, (one in each corner and two between the corner boxes along each side). The boxes should be numbered 1 through 10 starting anywhere. Then a skull and crossbones, or an X, or the words dead box, etc. is drawn inside the remaining inner square. Players should mark a throwing spot on the ground a reasonable distance away from the square and choose a throwing order.

Object: To be the first to successfully complete the entire round.

Play: The first player stands or sits on the throwing spot and attempts to flick his or her bottle cap into the box marked as "1". All throws are made from the marked spot. If that player successfully lands the cap in the "1" box, he or she goes again, this time shooting for box "2", then box "3", and so on. As soon as that player is unsuccessful, his or her turn is over and the next person repeats this process. On their next turn, players resume where they had missed on the previous turn. If one's bottle cap lands in the "dead box" (the very middle square), however, then that player's turn ends *and* that player must begin back at box "1" on the next turn. The winner is the first to finish the round by landing his or her bottle cap successfully in box "10".

Personal Comments: Remember, the smaller you draw the outside boxes, the more challenging it will be, and the bigger you draw the "dead box", the more challenging it will be. So as you get better, draw the boxes differently to make it more difficult. This game is much harder than it sounds because caps bounce and roll quite a lot. Practice and get good.

Down Down Down[2]

Number of kids: at least 2

Ages: any

Time allotted: 20 minutes or more

Space /Area: any open area of grass

Equipment: one tennis ball

Description:

Startup: Players should spread out evenly in a circle and set up so they can toss the ball to each other.

Object: To be the last person remaining.

Play: One player starts with the ball and throws it to the next player in the circle. If a successful catch is made, there is no penalty and the catcher then throws the ball to the next person, and so on. Penalties occur when a ball is dropped or a throw is so bad that it is uncatchable. When a player incurs his or her first penalty, everyone should say "Down on one knee". That player must then get down on one knee and continue playing from that position. The second penalty is "Down on two knees", then "Down on one elbow", then one's fourth penalty means elimination from the game. Each time a player incurs a penalty, that player must follow what is said and get down on one knee, then two, then one elbow, then elimination. That player continues to catch and pass as before, but must do so in the said position, making it more and more difficult. When a player is eliminated, players remain exactly where they are and play continues. This continues until only one player is left.

Personal Comments: This can be a blast to watch and to play. It is harder, but actually more fun being down on your knees or knees and one elbow. This is good catching and throwing practice and is very challenging and fun!

Frisbee™ Golf

Number of kids: 1; 2 or more for competition

Ages: any

Time allotted: 30 minutes or more

Space /Area: a large fairly open area, such as a large yard, several adjacent yards, or a field.

Equipment: one Frisbee for each child

Description:

Startup: Players should choose a Frisbee and find a starting point.

Object: To hit the chosen target in the least number of throws.

Play: One player chooses an object, such as a tree trunk, as the goal for the first hole. As in golf, players then take turns throwing their Frisbees towards the destination. Each player tries to hit the target in the least number of throws. Once each player has reached the destination, the winner of the hole chooses the next target. Turns may also be taken in choosing the next hole. A course of a pre-determined number of holes may be played, or simply play hole-by-hole. The winner, as in regular golf, is the player that takes the least total throws or wins the most holes.

Personal comments: Tons of fun and can really be played anywhere by anyone. I highly recommend this game. Make long holes and launch that Frisbee hard!!

Variant: Soccer Golf: In this game, players should follow the same rules, but should kick a soccer ball instead of throwing a Frisbee.

Homerun Derby

Number of kids: at least 3

Ages: 8 and up

Time allotted: 30 minutes or more

Space /Area: any large open area

Equipment: one baseball bat and one or more balls to hit (can be baseballs in a baseball field or tennis balls for more urban areas) and a baseball mitt for each child

Description:

Startup: Players should find a large area in which to play and choose a home run line.

Object: To hit the most home runs.

Play: Once a playing field is picked, one person chooses to bat first and one person chooses to pitch. Everyone else spreads around the field and helps to retrieve balls. When everyone is ready, the pitcher throws the first pitch to the batter. The pitches must be soft and easy to hit. If the batter hits a homerun on that pitch, the batter begins to count his or her home run total. If the batter hits anything but a homerun, he or she receives one out. That batter hits until he or she receives a prechosen number of outs (usually 3, 5, or 10). The next batter then steps up and pitcher's may switch as well. Each batter should remember how many homeruns they hit during their round. After everyone has had a chance to bat, the round ends. Player's can hit as many rounds as they desire and the winner is the person who has the highest tally of homeruns.

Personal comments: This is a great time because all you do is crank the ball as hard as you can. Good to get out aggression, work on baseball hitting, and just to go have some fun.

Horse

Number of kids: at least 2

Ages: any

Time allotted: 25 minutes or more

Space /Area: any basketball area

Equipment: one basketball

Description:

Startup: Players should find an area to play and choose a shooting order.

Object: To be the last player remaining.

Play: The first player starts with the basketball and may shoot any type of shot from any place on the court. If that player misses, it becomes the next person's turn to do the same. If a player makes his or her shot, the next person in line must then make the same shot. If this player matches that shot, the next player must make the shot, and so on. If everyone matches the shot, the original shooter chooses a new shot. If anyone is trying to match a shot and misses, the player who missed earns a letter. The first letter a player earned is "H", then "O", then "R", then "S", and lastly "E". Once someone has earned HORSE, that player is out of the game.

    Once someone earns a letter, the original shot no longer has to be matched, and the next person in line shoots a new shot (for example, if person 1 makes a shot then person 2 fails to make that shot, person 2 earns a letter and it is then person's 3 turn to shoot from anywhere).** Play continues until everyone but one player has spelled "HORSE". This last player is the winner. The only other rule is that the same person should not shoot from the same place where he or she made a previous shot.

**Some people play that everyone must try to match the shot and can earn a letter, but the former variation is more common.

Personal comments: Works on basketball skills and is fun and competitive. Be creative with your shots and go for crazy stuff, it can be even more fun that way.

Jacks

Number of kids: at least 2

Ages: any

Time allotted: 20 minutes or more

Space /Area: a porch or a small cement or paved area

Equipment: one small bouncy ball and several jacks (these can be cheaply bought or any small, easily scoopable objects can be substituted).

Description:

Startup: Players should find an area to play and determine an order.

Object: To pick up the most jacks each round.

Play: The first player spreads the jacks out in a small area on the ground. That player must then drop the bouncy ball. The same player must then pick up one jack and catch the ball before it bounces more than once. If he or she fails to do this, the turn is over. If successful, that player repeats the process but must pick up two jacks. The next drop he or she must pick up three, and so on until an attempt is failed. The next player then does the same. Several rounds are played and the winner is the person who got up to the highest number of jacks.

Personal Comments: An easy game, but an addicting one. Start playing, get good, and you'll want to play more. Good for setting records and trying to break them.

Lawn Darts

Number of kids: at least 2

Ages: any

Time allotted: 30 minutes or more

Space /Area: an open strip of grass

Equipment: two hoops (hula-hoop size) and 3 to 5 lawn darts. Lawn darts can be bought or a number of tossable objects can be substituted for them (e.g. sticks or balls or even old shoes).

Description:

Startup: Players should spread the hoops out a reasonable distance and set them on the ground. If there are more than two players, teams should be formed. Each player or team then stands behind a hoop.

Object: To score the most points.

Play: One player or team starts with all the lawn darts and tosses them towards the opponents' hoop. A player must toss from BEHIND his or her own hoop. After all the darts have been tossed, one point is awarded for each dart that has settled inside the hoop. The opposing team then tosses the darts in the same fashion. The winner is the first to reach a pre-determined number (usually 10, 15, or 20).

Option: If enough darts are present (so each team has a set), an alternative set of rules can be put in place. Each team throws their darts at the same time. A team then scores by making a larger number of darts then their opponent. For example, if during the first round of tossing, team 1 successfully lands all five darts in team 2's hoop, and team 2 only lands two darts, then team 1 would score the difference of 3 points. Play also goes until one team reaches a pre-determined number (usually 10, 15, or 20).

Personal Comments: Easy and tons of fun. Anyone can play. This game takes some practice and gets more fun as you improve. Develop your own style of throwing and go for it!

Lawn Golf

Number of kids: 1; 2 or more for competition

Ages: 8 and up

Time allotted: 30 minutes or more

Space /Area: a large fairly open area, such as a large yard, several adjacent yards, or a field.

Equipment: one golf club and tennis ball for each player

Description:

Startup: Players should choose a golf club, grab a tennis ball, and find a starting point.

Object: To hit the chosen target in the least number of strokes.

Play: One player chooses an object, such as a tree, as the target for the first hole. As in real golf, the players then take turns hitting their ball towards the destination. Each player tries to hit the target in the least number of strokes. Once each player has reached the destination, the winner of the hole (the player with the least strokes) chooses the next target. Players may also take turns in choosing the next hole, especially if a tie occurs. A course of a pre-determined number of holes may be played, or participants can simply play hole-by-hole. The winner, as in regular golf, is the player that takes the least total strokes or wins the most holes.

Personal comments: Tons of fun and can really be played anywhere by anyone. I highly suggest this game. Just go play for fun. You do not even have to count strokes. Make long holes and enjoy smacking the ball and wandering after it!!

Line Club Bowl[3]

Number of kids: at least 2

Ages: any

Time allotted: 40 minutes or more

Space /Area: an open strip of short grass

Equipment: 3 pins and one ball of choice per player or team. Pins can be anything that could topple over like bowling pins, such as small cones.

Description:

Startup: Players should determine a starting line and set up the pins a reasonable distance from it. Pins should be set up in a triangular pattern. Players then choose an order to bowl.

Object: To have the highest score after 10 rounds or to reach a certain score first.

Play: Players take turns bowling from behind the determined starting line. For each throw, one point is scored for knocking down a pin, 3 points are scored for knocking down two pins, and 5 points are scored for knocking down all 3 pins in ONE throw. Players continue to take turns bowling and keep track of their score. One twist is that the pins are only set back up after all three pins have been knocked down! If a player only knocks down one pin, it stays down for every round until all 3 pins are knocked down. Pins are then set back up. The game ends when one person or team reaches a set number of points. 10 rounds may also be bowled, with the winner having the highest total.

Personal Comments: A very simple bowling game, but a fun one. Takes some skill to hit the third pin when two are already down. Can promote fun team bonding and some good skills. Easy to set up and is fun for hours!!

Variant: Stake Target Bowl[3]: In this game, one stake is put into the ground. Each bowler has several balls. They takes turns rolling from behind the predetermined line. One point is awarded for each time the stake is hit. The winner has the most points at the end of 10 rounds.

Long Ball[3]

Number of kids: at least 5

Ages: 8 and up

Time allotted: 30 minutes or more

Space /Area: any large open area

Equipment: one baseball bat and one or more balls to hit (can be baseballs in a baseball field or tennis balls for more urban areas) and a baseball mitt for each child

Description:

Startup: Players should find a big area in which to play and choose one or more bases that are required to touch (usually just one, but can be two or three).

Object: To hit the most home runs.

Play: Once a playing field is picked, one person chooses to bat first and one person chooses to pitch. One players should be a catcher as well. Everyone else spreads around the field. When everyone is ready, the pitcher throws the first pitch to the batter. The pitches must be soft and easy to hit. If the batter hits the ball, he or she must run to the base(s) chosen and make it home safely without being tagged out or forced out at home. If successful, the batter earns one homerun. Otherwise, any other hit (foul ball, caught fly, tagged out, forced out, etc.) results in one out. That batter hits until he or she receives a prechosen number of outs (usually 3, 5, or 10). The next batter then steps up and pitcher's may switch as well. Each player should remember how many runs they hit. After everyone has had a chance to bat, the round ends. Player's can hit as many rounds as they desire and the winner is the person who has the highest tally of homeruns.

Personal Comments: Good variant of homerun derby! All the same fun or derby with some extra running, fielding, exercise, and skills. Good for any baseball fan.

Variant: This game can be played with teams as well.

Marbles

Number of kids: at least 2

Ages: any

Time allotted: 20 minutes or more

Space /Area: a small, rough surfaced area, such as bare ground (packed dirt or sand).

Equipment: one "shooter" (large marble) and the desired number of small marbles for each child

Description:

Startup: Players should draw a circle on the ground, roughly 18 inches across, to designate the playing area. They should then spread their marbles randomly within the circle.

Object: To knock the most marbles out of the circle.

Play: Each player takes turns shooting their "shooter" into the circle in an attempt to knock small marbles out of the circle. This is done by sticking the marble on top of the hand and flicking it with the thumb. The player's hand must stay out of the circle while shooting. Any marble successfully knocked out goes into that player's pile. Once all the marbles are shot out of the circle, the player with the largest pile wins.

Personal Comments: A game that kids do not bother to play much anymore, but is truly fun, especially after some practice! Go give it a *shot*.

Mother May I

Number of kids: at least 3

Ages: any

Time allotted: 20 minutes or more

Space /Area: a long path of any surface

Equipment: none

Description:

Startup: Players should designate a playing area and choose one person to be the "mother". The mother stands at one end of the playing area and everyone else starts at the other end.

Object: To be the first player to reach the end where the mother is standing.

Play: Each player take turns asking the mother to move forward. They phrase questions in the form "Mother may I.….?" and request to take any number of baby steps, regular steps, big steps, leaps, etc. For example, "Mother may I take two big steps?". The mother then says yes or no. If a request is granted, that player moves accordingly. If a request is denied that player must take one step backwards. The first player to reach the mother is then the mother for the next round. A boy at the end of the field should be referred to as father.

Personal comments: Not the most high paced action, but it is fun to see what you can get away with and what you cannot. Be smart with how much you ask for!

Paper Plane Contest

Number of kids: at least 2

Ages: any

Time allotted: at least 20 minutes

Space /Area: any open area

Equipment: a few sheets of paper for each child

Description:

Startup: Everyone should have some semi-firm paper to use (computer paper works well).

Object: To build a plane that will fly the farthest.

Play: Everyone can build one, two, or even three planes (players' choice). As long as players use only one sheet of paper per plane, they can fold it in any way they please. Once all the planes are constructed, players should find a starting line and take turns throwing their planes. If desired, players can take more than one throw with each plane by using an object to mark their longest throw. Each player takes the decided number of throws with each of their planes. The winner is the person who had the plane that flew the farthest. Fold new planes or keep old ones and try it again!

Personal comments: A very simple game, but can be a lot of fun, especially for younger kids, or kids who love paper airplanes. You can keep the best planes to fly in multiple contests or can start over each time. Be creative and try different folding techniques and see if you can beat your best record.

Pottsie[1]

Number of kids: at least 2

Ages: any

Time allotted: 30 minutes or more

Space /Area: a large paved area that can be drawn on with chalk

Equipment: one piece of chalk and a ball that bounces well

Description:

Startup: One player should draw ten squares along the ground (about 2 feet wide) and write one category in each. Categories should be familiar to all players, such as states, candy bars, and animals. Each player should find a rock to toss and an order of players should be made. A throwing line should also be marked about 5 feet back from the boxes.

Object: To finish the course first.

Play: The first player stands on the throwing line and must toss his or her rock into the first square. If successful, that player attempts to run the course. Running the course is done by bouncing the ball and catching it once in each square. As this is done, the player must say aloud a member of the category that is written in the box where the ball is bouncing. If the player completes all ten boxes successfully, he or she gets to go again. That player returns to the throwing line and tries to toss the rock into the next box. A player's turn ends when the rock is not tossed into the correct box or the course is not completed correctly. Course errors include dropping the ball, bouncing it on a line or in the wrong box, or failing to name a correct member of a category. Each turn, a player begins where he or she made an error on the last turn. The first player to make it through all ten boxes is the winner.

Personal comments: This is a good hopscotch variant. It takes creativity as well as good coordination. Best for younger children, but can by played by anyone.

Rears Up

Number of kids: at least 3

Ages: 10 and up

Time allotted: 20 minutes or more

Space/Area: a small area of any surface

Equipment: one soccer ball or hackey sack

Description:

Startup: One person starts with the ball and everyone gets into a circle.

Object: To avoid receiving letters.

Play: The player that has the ball begins juggling it (hitting into the air and keeping it there). Hands and arms are never allowed to be used, but using any other body part is fine. The person who starts the ball in the air may immediately knock it over to someone else or hit it a few times. There is no limit to how many consecutive times a player can hit the ball. The ball continues to be passed from person to person in the air until a player causes the ball to drop to the ground. This can happen if a player botches a pass that came to him or her, or if someone's pass is unplayable. If a player cause the ball to drop, that player gains one letter. Players are always responsible to play the ball if it comes close to them. Failure to do so also results in a letter. A player earns an "R" the first time he or she causes the ball to drop, then "E", and so on until "REARS" is spelled. The first person to spell this is the loser.

    The game may end there and start over, or for older players, this rule may be played: The losing player must turn around and place his or her hands on a wall. The rest of the players take one turn either throwing or kicking the ball at this player (depending on what type of ball was used). Then a new round begins. Each new round, everyone starts with no letters.

Personal comments: Little kids probably shouldn't play the optional rule, nor should people who cannot take being hit by a ball. Player's should do this for fun only, not to hurt anyone. This rule is done for fun, but can get a little ugly. Just play for fun, try not to kill each other. This game as a whole works on coordination and dribbling skills and is a blast. Just as fun without the optional rule!

Soccer Croquet

Number of kids: 2 or more

Ages: any

Time allotted: 20 minutes or more

Space/Area: a small grassy area

Equipment: one soccer ball for each player and several plastic cones (or something similar)

Description:

Startup: Players make a croquet course using cones. This is done by setting up a series of cones in the grassy area. The cones should be set in pairs. The paired cones should be about two feet apart, so that a soccer ball can be easily kicked between them. The pairs can be spread around the course in any given manner. Players should choose an order of play. A beginning point should also be designated.

Object: To be the first player to finish the course.

Play: The first player set his or her ball on the beginning point. This player then attempts to kick his or her ball through the first pair of cones. If successful, this players then kicks towards the second pair of cones, and so forth. As soon as a player fails to kick his or her ball through the next pair of cones, that player's turn is finished. The next player then does the same. At the end of a player's turn, his or her ball remains where it is and is kicked again the next round. Players must finish the course, turn around, and then come back through it in the reverse direction. The winner is the first player to return to the beginning point. If balls contact, there is no penalty. The balls are simply played from where they lay.

Personal Comments: This game takes skill and precision. It is fun, competitive, and works on soccer skills. Try turning the cones sideways, etc. to make the course more challenging. You can even play around trees and other objects as well. This game is easy to play and lots of fun. Give it a try!

Throw for Distance[3]

Number of kids: at least 2

Ages: any

Time allotted: 20 minutes or more

Space /Area: a long open area of grass or field

Equipment: each player needs an equal amount of the chosen throwing objects (usually balls of any kind, but other safe objects, such as Frisbees can be used)

Description:

Startup: Players should select all the objects to be thrown (for example: 2 tennis balls, two different sized footballs, one soccer ball, three Frisbees, and one lawn darts apiece). Then a throw line is chosen and all the objects are set behind the line. The players then mark off lines at any distance down the field. Throwing past the first line will be worth one point, past the second is worth two points, etc. Usually 5 lines are drawn, but this can vary.

Object: To score the most points.

Play: Play begins with the players standing behind the throw line. The players then take turns throwing an object as far as they can. Each then throws the next object and so on until all objects have been thrown. One or more attempts may be agreed upon with hard to throw objects, such as Frisbees. All the points earned by each player are added and the player with the most points wins.

Personal Comments: Extremely fun and simple. Try all sorts of balls. You'll be surprised how much variance their can be in who can throw best with different objects. Try this out and let 'em rip!!

Untangle

Number of kids: at least 5

Ages: any

Time allotted: 20 minutes or more

Space /Area: a small open area of grass or soft surface

Equipment: none

Description:

Startup: Everyone gets into a circle. Each player then simultaneously and randomly reaches into the circle and grabs one hand of two different people.

Object: To untangle the mess that has just been formed.

Play: In this game, anything goes except players CANNOT let go of the persons' hands they are holding, not even for a second! Players may do anything else to attempt to get free and eventually they should return to an untangled circle where no one's arms are crossed. This is a group goal and everyone wins!

Personal comments: This SOUNDS easy, but is really messy and a ton of fun. The more people you have, the harder and more entertaining it is. Be creative. This takes a lot of weaving, stepping over and under, etc. It can be tough, but no cheating! Go find a bunch of people and get tangled!

Water Balloon Toss

Number of kids: at least 2 teams of 2

Ages: any

Time allotted: 10 minutes or more

Space /Area: a decent sized grass area

Equipment: one water balloon per team for each game played

Description:

Startup: Players should pair off and each team gets one water balloon. The teammates face each other and get in one big line, as follows:

```
1     2     3     4…..and so on
1     2     3     4…..and so on
```

Where the "1"s are a team, the "2"s are a team, and so on

Object: To be the only remaining team with an unpopped balloon.

Play: Everyone on one side starts with their team's water balloon. Each player then passes their balloon to their teammate. If the balloon did not pop, whoever just passed their balloon takes a big step back. The balloon is then passed back, and the thrower again takes a step back. Each team must pass and step back in unison to ensure each team stays the same distance apart. If a team's balloon breaks at any time, they are out of the game. The winner is proclaimed when there is only remaining team with an unpopped balloon. Players can switch or keep partners and try it again as many times as desired.

Personal comments: Good for a really hot day. Gets you a little wet and lets you have some great competition and fun!

References

(cited in superscript)

1. Macguire, J. (1990). <u>Hopscotch, Hangman, Hot Potato, & Ha Ha Ha: A Rulebook of Children's Games.</u> Simon & Schuster: New York

2. Nieboer, G. Games Kids Play. 2002. Online. <www.gameskidsplay.net>

3. Richardson, H.A. (1966). <u>Games for Junior and Senior High Schools</u>. Burgess Publishing: Minneapolis, MN.

4. Smith, C.F. (1952). <u>Boy Scout Games</u>. Boy Scouts of America: New York.

About the Author

My true knowledge of outdoor games comes from personal experience, not only in teaching and supervising games, but playing and creating them as well! Growing up in a neighborhood that thrived on these games has allowed me to write excellent descriptions and enjoyable and useful personal comments on each game. I received my B.A. from the University of Notre Dame with majors in psychology and preprofessional studies. I am currently researching child development for my Ph.D. at the University of Louisville. In my years of psychology research, I have spent uncountable hours working with children of all ages. I have also spent numerous summers teaching and coaching tennis, in which creating and playing games was essential.

CPSIA information can be obtained at www.ICGtesting.com
Printed in the USA
BVOW051907221211

279044BV00001B/16/A

9 781418 422264